Finding Hope Again

Peter Millar, who was formerly Warden of Iona Abbey, is
a minister of the Church of Scotland and a member of the
Iona Community. He and his late wife, Dr Dorothy Millar,
worked for many years in the Church of South India. He is
author of the *Iona Pilgrim Guide*, *An Iona Prayer Book*
and *Waymarks: signposts to discovering God's presence in
the world*, also published by the Canterbury Press.

D0493902

Praise for Peter Millar's *Waymarks*,
published by the Canterbury Press:

'*Waymarks* is a book full of the rich experiences of life, of
stories and people and how we are all connected to God.'
Magnet

'a marvellous resource for inspiration and reflection . . .
all who read it will have their spiritual awareness
deepened and their lives enriched.'
Revd Norman Shanks
Leader of the Iona Community

Finding Hope Again

Journeying through sorrow and beyond

Peter Millar

CANTERBURY
PRESS
Norwich

© Peter W. Millar 2003

First published in 2003 by
The Canterbury Press Norwich
(a publishing imprint of Hymns Ancient & Modern Limited,
a registered charity)
St Mary's Works, St Mary's Plain,
Norwich, Norfolk, NR3 3BH

www.scm-canterburypress.co.uk

British Library Cataloguing in Publication data

A catalogue record for this book is available
from the British Library

ISBN 1–85311–438–3

Typeset by Rowland Phototypesetting Limited,
Bury St Edmunds, Suffolk
Printed in Great Britain by
Bookmarque Ltd, Croydon, Surrey

For Eldon and Ange,
Tim, and Sulekha
who give me so much hope.

Contents

Contents

Introduction

It's easy to give up on hope, especially when we are in a bad space. When life gets on top of us it's not too difficult to give hope the body-swerve. We just can't believe that hope is anywhere, either in ourselves, or in the world or in God, or in all three mixed together. What we do see are life's dark, never-ending tunnels. It may be that we are suddenly made redundant, or discover that we have been abandoned by the person who seemed closest to us, or the doctor has just told us that we need investigative surgery or our kid is going to pieces, or . . . or . . .

And all around us, a lot of the world seems to be in bad space as well. Ordinary folk in their tens of thousands are starving, while governments spend billions on arms; Aids kills children who have everything to live for; and the planet itself cries out from wounds that seem impossible to heal. It all boggles the mind, and stirs within us feelings which are the very opposite of hope.

And in the midst of all this, I didn't wake up one morning and thought it would be good idea to put together a book about finding hope again! What I did do was to wake up one spring morning and less than an hour later find the person I loved most, my wife, lying on the bathroom floor, dying from a massive blood clot. And in the months that followed I knew what it was to live in a very dark tunnel, as did my three children. It was utter darkness. I did not feel angry or bitter, just overwhelmed by grief, lost in a sorrow that had ambushed my whole existence.

For the twenty-seven years of our marriage, Dorothy and I had worked as a team, in various parts of the world. In India, where we lived for many years with our family, we had seen suffering and death on a daily basis. Yet when it came to my own door-step I was engulfed in a sadness which carried an intensity I could hardly bear. Sometimes I felt completely unable to get through the day, let alone the night. And within a few weeks of Dorothy's death, a close friend who was staying in our home and who had come to comfort us, was killed in a road accident just a mile from the house. It seemed that the dark tunnel would go on for ever.

But just as death can come without even a moment's warning, the tiniest glimmers of hope seem to sneak in under a crack by the back door. Like death or suffering, they too can come unannounced, even in the darkest nights. And it's because I believe that, I wanted to write about it and to invite friends who have been in similar dark tunnels themselves, or who have experienced these small moments of hope, to share in it.

This is not to say that I believe in 'easy answers' or in a God who suddenly swoops down from on high to give me special comfort in my hour of crisis. What I do believe is that my slow and fragile journey into finding hope again is part and parcel of a mystery which, although I cannot comprehend it, is itself rooted in the heart of a God who has not abandoned, and never will abandon, his creation.

I am still in grief and will miss Dorothy for the rest of my life on earth. Life for me is not the same, and it would be crazy to say that it was. I know that thousands of others who have lost loved ones are in a similar situation. For one reason or other, our lives have been turned upside-down and inside-out – through bereavement, through the break-up of a relationship, through illness. There are hundreds of reasons – and often our pain is hidden well away from others, even our dearest ones.

Primo Levi, who was a prisoner in a German concentration camp during the Second World War, has recorded in his writing something of the unspeakable horrors which he witnessed. Yet in these situations of monumental human cruelty, he also saw signs of what he calls 'unavoidable hope', the reality that even in the worst hell-holes, a 'living hope' emerged. And it was real hope, not a fantasy – enabling people to survive another minute, another hour, another day.

In our work around the world, Dorothy and I often saw evidence of this 'unavoidable hope' breaking through in circumstances which seemed utterly hopeless. It was hope in the midst of wounds, and because of that it became prophetic hope which was able to affirm others in their depths. We can find new purpose for our lives by these songs of hope, even though we may have little knowledge of the actual circumstances which gave them birth. And they are all around us, day by day.

I would like this book to be 'a song of hope'. A book which speaks of that kind of hope which emerges within the heart of our dark tunnels. For if hope does not come from these hard places, it is only a superficial optimism which will not sustain us, or our world. I know this from my own experience. There are no easy answers or quick fixes – a truth which is more than obvious in the present global situation. Yet while recognizing that reality, it would be heartening if even a word or a phrase in these pages mirrors your own situation and gives you a fresh glimmer of hope. Or maybe two glimmers! For the story of one person is in a sense our common story – however different the outward circumstances. I have always believed that in the heart of God we are intimately connected, which is what makes possible our essential solidarity with one another.

As I try, falteringly, to open up my own humanity to God, I think of the hope which Jesus Christ offered, and continues to offer, to our divided world. And as I reflect upon Christ's life on this earth, I become aware that this hope certainly did not come from a comfortable place, but from one which was often framed by abandonment and loneliness. Yet it was real. It was also life-giving, and as we look back over the last twenty centuries of Christian history we see how this gift of hope has transformed individuals and whole communities. It is an ever-moving hope, without boundaries – at its heart both a mystery and a strength.

In my own pilgrimage I try to remain open to God's surprises. That is not always easy, and some days I feel low and uncertain. Yet I can honestly say that something of this Christ-filled hope has touched my life as I travel along the dark tunnels. Not every day, but on some days, that hope about which the Bible speaks is my companion. A gentle companion whose hands are on my shoulder when my eyes are filled with tears, and my heart laments both for myself and our wounded world. The God of ancient calm who touches my empty spaces when I am vulnerable enough to meet him. That 'whispering in my heart' which re-connects me with hope, and with my sisters and brothers wherever they are on this amazing planet.

Part One
Sorrow

A morning in March

It was clear and frosty that early March morning in the Scottish Highlands. There was a light covering of snow on the mountains around our village on the banks of the fast-flowing Spey, and the aconites and snowdrops, these first heralds of spring, were still asleep. It was Friday 9 March, and the weather forecast predicted a sunny day for our part of Inverness-shire. On a small stone wall by the kitchen widow, our friendly robin, waiting for his breakfast from Dorothy, had been joined by many friends.

The village of Laggan has a history stretching back through the centuries, but in these last few years it has also come to be known as 'Glenbogle' because the TV series *Monarch of the Glen* is filmed there. It is a place of great natural beauty, in all seasons. In late winter and early spring there is a quality of light in the valley which always reaffirms my belief that our natural world is threaded through with mystery, and that there is only a thin line between the material and the spiritual. The forests, rivers and mountains, all in their own particular way, sing of the glory of God – a truth announced by monks in the Celtic church as they crossed these same Highland hills almost 1,500 years ago.

It was just after 8 a.m. Dorothy gave me a smile and wave from our bedroom window as I began to climb the steep path leading into the woods behind our cottage, which is named after the island of Iona off the west coast of Scotland, where Columba set up his famous monastery in the sixth century. By my side was our faithful black labrador, Kuti. Together we went up through the pines, larches and birches until we could look over the valley to the mountains, which stretch in all directions as far as the eye can see. These ancient hills which, in any season, can bring to our frenetic minds a quiet certitude.

And as I walked I thought about some words, which I had read ten minutes earlier. They were written by a Jewish philosopher: 'Every moment can be a small door through which the Messiah may enter.' Was I open to that possibility in my own life? Did I live with an expectant heart? Or had I become stale with the passing of the years? Did I just take God for granted? Was I prepared to take new risks in my journey of faith? Many questions flitted through my head on that early morning walk. And as I thought about them, Kuti was discovering exciting new smells at every turn. At least there was no doubt that she was open to new experiences – every day!

Some weeks earlier, Dorothy and I had returned from Australia where we had been working for a year with the Wellspring Community. This ecumenical Christian community, committed to an engaged spirituality, was started about ten years ago. Its founders were inspired by the Iona Community of which I have been a member for many years. Although we travelled extensively throughout Australia, meeting and sharing with many people, our base had been in the Mt Druitt area of western Sydney. In that vast section of public housing, which carries many of the markers of urban deprivation, we had learned so much – not least from our Aboriginal neighbours.

The Community in Australia had invited us to return to

work with them, and we were in the midst of making plans for the journey. Later in the day we would be checking out some flight details. Yet our departure for Australia still seemed a long time ahead, and before that we would be celebrating the graduations of two of our children. Life was full, and I felt grateful to God for all the ways in which we had been blessed as a family. I stood in silence and gazed over the mountain ridges. And then in that golden morning stillness, as the mist slowly rose from the hills, I heard a shout coming up from the valley below.

It came again. It was our son Tim (who was back at home for a couple of days) calling for me from near our cottage. I remember little of that race through the woods with Kuti running behind. Moments seemed like hours. 'Phone for an ambulance! Mum has collapsed!' shouted Tim, even before we had reached the house. As he ran back upstairs I phoned, then followed him to be with Dorothy.

South India had been our home for many years and its people were still in our hearts. Living in that complex and beautiful land had transformed our understanding of life. Our way of perceiving suffering had also been radically altered. We had seen the face of sudden illness countless times, often standing by anxious relatives, themselves the victims of poverty and injustice, as they watched a loved one become critically ill in a matter of minutes. And many times I had seen Dorothy's sari-clad figure gently holding a mother and father as they buried their young child in a shallow grave, as the fireball which was the evening sun slid down behind the palms.

And in all these situations, it was Dorothy's serenity which had brought comfort to people. It was an inner calmness which permeated all her actions and brought courage to others, often in circumstances which were framed in misery, gut-wrenching poverty and apparent hopelessness. Even though her cultural background was different, our Indian friends intuitively discerned that in Dorothy they had a person who walked with them in their depths and who valued their wisdom and defiant hope. She was someone who knew what Joanna Macy meant when she wrote: 'You have been through many dyings and know in your heartbeat and bones the precarious and exquisite balance of life.'

'We are here with you,' Tim and I said to Dorothy again and again as we knelt by her still body. With gentle tenderness, Tim, who was then a final-year medical student, was trying to revive his mum. By now a doctor and our local ambulance were both heading for Laggan. They would be with us in minutes. Several of our wonderful neighbours, aware that something was wrong, were rushing to the house. Kuti was by our side – expectant as ever. Downstairs the radio was telling of the latest developments in the Palestinian–Israeli conflict, and at the back door the birds were still waiting for breakfast.

And in the midst of it all, Dorothy, who had watched and waited with so many others as they moved into their final journey on earth, was now herself beginning to experience that ultimate new dawning. As Tim and I held her close, her extraordinarily creative life – permeated with love, laughter and wisdom – was painlessly and effortlessly travelling into the wider possibilities of God. In medical terms, a rapidly-moving blood clot was causing her breathing to come to an end. The Dorothy who was the heartbeat of our family and whom we loved at such depth, was now on a journey without our immediate companionship. Silently, suddenly and without even a moment of warning, death had become her companion – and ours. We held one another in love – three of us, on a bathroom floor, in a Highland cottage, on a morning in March.

And then the words that brought it home. Tim's quiet voice: 'Mum's gone.' And across Dorothy's calm body, our eyes met – and our endless tears started to flow. It was a new day in ways that we had never dreamed of, or even imagined. And outside our cottage, as an empty ambulance headed back through the village, I heard our neighbours crying.

By the fast-flowing Spey

In a green place
Of quiet light
By the waters of the
Fast-flowing Spey,
Watched over by ancient hills
And gentle woods,
Your body lies.
Close by those
Strong church walls
That held your prayers,
Your songs,
Your laughter
And inspiring words
Which drew us
Close to God.

The seasons change
But still you lie
Next to Ian,
And Davie,
And Margaret
And Peter
And Alastair
And Mary
And Dougal

Sorrow

Who
Like you,
Knew and loved
These ancient
Highland hills,
And called them home.

Your gaze
Is cosmic now,
Far wider than before,
Illumining
Our days
Despite
Our tears;
Inviting us
To see
The face of God,
And journey on.

Dorothy – a gentle revolutionary

> Who brings about peace
> is called
> the companion of God
> in the work of creation.
>
> *Jewish saying*

> God help us to change,
> To change ourselves, and to change our world.
> To know the need for it.
> To deal with the pain of it.
> To feel the joy of it.
> To undertake the journey
> without understanding the destination,
> the art of gentle revolution.
>
> *Michael Leunig*[1]

> God is found where there is fire in your heart.
>
> *Matthew Fox*

Initially I was reluctant to write this piece about Dorothy, for she never thought of herself as a special person, and was always encouraging others to celebrate their gifts and talents. Yet for many people around the world she was a 'bearer of hope' – in fact, 'a gentle revolutionary'. Michael

Leunig's words, which I copied from her journal, capture some essential element in her life's journey.

Born in Calcutta, from her childhood she valued the variety and exuberance of Bengali culture, never imagining that later in life her own home would be in India for several years. Her family later returned from India to Scotland, and then went to New Zealand, where her interest in Maori traditions began to develop. With that appreciation went a questioning of certain Western social values and easily-arrived-at Christian belief.

Her initial post-doctoral work as a bacteriologist was with the distinguished New Zealand scientist Molly Marples who was at that time an international authority on the ecology of the human skin. With Marples, Dorothy became involved in research projects in the Pacific Islands, and while working with families in the Cook Islands became drawn to their strong sense of community and awareness of the sacred in all things.

Back in London, she continued her scientific work, and with Professor Bill Noble co-authored a seminal work, *Microbiology of the Human Skin*. Her numerous publications and pioneering research on the ecology of the human skin brought membership and later fellowship of the Royal College of Pathologists. It was at this time that Dorothy took up posts at Glasgow University and at Glasgow's Royal Infirmary – a teaching hospital not far from my parish in the East End of that great city.

After our marriage and despite the demands of her work in this country and overseas, Dorothy became closely involved with the problems facing families in the East End – unemployment, poor health, extremely bad housing and lack of opportunity for all ages, to name but a few! And through this growing awareness of urban deprivation, her

Christian faith became much more radical – a change which in turn gave birth to her conviction that injustice, wherever it was found, must be challenged. Yet this radical faith was firmly earthed in a faithfulness to listening to God – to being open to the Spirit in all of its surprising turns.

A prayer which expressed something of this ongoing pilgrimage with God kept reappearing in Dorothy's journals:

> God of ancient calm, let your peace still us:
> God of fearful storm, fill us with your awe:
> God of lonely plains, touch the empty spaces
> Within us,
> Where we are vulnerable enough
> To meet you.

From the urban poverty and rich friendships of Glasgow's East End we moved to another kind of poverty in South India, where we worked for eleven years. Dorothy's sari-clad figure soon became a familiar sight in some of the villages of Tamil Nadu and in the poorer areas of the vast city of Chennai which was then known as Madras. It was in Chennai that our daughter Sulekha was born. Our sons, Eldon and Tim, attended a school near our home, and one of the excitements of the year was when we travelled by train together, in the sweltering heat of high summer, into the glorious high mountains of South India.

Even in the highest temperatures Dorothy's energy appeared to be limitless, and some of the projects which she established with Indian colleagues were both pioneering and visionary. Yet she never saw herself as a person coming from the 'developed world' bearing 'answers' to

India's problems – either in relation to her Christianity or to her scientific and medical knowledge. She was always slightly suspicious of certain types of Christian evangelism, which seemed unwilling to embrace the complexities of an ancient and multi-faced culture. She also believed that international aid work had to be done with great sensitivity to local circumstances, and that while financial assistance was necessary in the fight against injustice, it must be recognized as only part of the solution.

Her love of India's ancient traditions is clearly evidenced in her writing and in the many talks which she gave over the years. Like our friend, the Benedictine monk Bede Griffiths, Dorothy knew that India had gifted to her life 'the other half of her soul'. That did not mean that her rational, scientific half was abandoned, but rather that her more vulnerable, intuitive side came into play. She found confirmation of this discovery of her 'other half' in some words of Ranier Maria Rilke:

> Be patient toward all that is unsolved in your heart
> and try to love the questions themselves.
> Do not seek answers, which cannot be given to you
> because you would not be able to live them.
>
> And the point is to live everything,
> live the questions now.
> Perhaps you will gradually,
> Without noticing it,
> live along some distant day,
> into the answer.

Seeing at first hand, in India, the horrific effects of wide-scale poverty, propelled her to campaign ceaselessly for the reduction of international debt and for fair-trading practices. In the early days of this work, few governments were prepared to take seriously the arguments in relation to global debt, but in the last years of her life Dorothy was encouraged by the wide response to this particular campaign, although she felt it was only in its initial stages.

Her own wide knowledge of the complexities which surround globalization challenged many people to think deeply about trade agreements, the power of multi-national companies and the role of governments in an interconnected world. In the last months of her life, when living in Australia, she included in her talks some words, written by an Aboriginal person, which she had seen on a poster in Brisbane. For Dorothy they encapsulated some fundamental aspects of our post-modern world in its ambiguity and contradiction:

> born in poverty:
> died in captivity:
> in an age of technology.

Her multiple experiences in India gave Dorothy an authoritative but compassionate voice when, on our return from there, we set up a small Christian centre, related to the Iona Community, in Scotland. The Columban House near the village of Newtonmore in the Highlands was both a retreat house and a base for reflection on global issues such as the environment, fair trade, international debt and the arms race. From this centre, Dorothy continued her international work while at the same time opening her heart to many individuals and families who arrived there in great pain and need. And it was in the simple prayer room at the Columban House that Dorothy first used these words from a Christian Aid liturgy:

> Loving God, take our hands,
> take our lives,
> ordinary as wheat or cornmeal,
> daily as bread –
> our stumbling generosity,
> our simple actions,
> and find them good enough
> to help prepare the feast
> for all your people.[2]

Some years later, when I was appointed Warden of Iona Abbey, Dorothy became a member of the Resident Group, who are responsible for welcoming the many thousands of people who visit the Iona Community on the island where the visionary and prophetic Columba established his monastery in 563 AD. Here again her creativity and engaged Christian faith challenged many who were searching for a Christianity that actually related to the modern world in all of its many puzzling, yet life-giving, pluralities. She valued this opportunity which the Iona Community had given her to walk with all kinds of people in their spiritual quest, for she was a pilgrim herself – one who could easily identify with Julia McGuinness's beautiful poem:

> Some people travel in straight lines:
> Sat in metal boxes, eyes ahead,
> Always mindful of the target,
> Moving in obedience to the coloured lights and
>   white lines,
> Mission accomplished at journey's end.

Some people travel round in circles:
Trudging in drudgery, eyes looking down,
Knowing only too well their daily unchanging round,
Moving in response to clock and habit,
Journey never finished yet never begun.

I want to travel in patterns of God's making:
Walking in wonder, gazing all around,
Knowing my destiny, though not my destination,
Moving to the rhythm of the surging of his spirit,
A journey which when life ends, in Christ has just begun.

From Iona we went to Australia to work with the Wellspring Community. This Community, which seeks to relate a radical, engaged Christianity to the realities of modern Australia, brought us into close contact with a great variety of people all over the country. Our base, in a poor part of western Sydney, enabled us to be alongside Aboriginal families who taught us much about their rich and ancient culture.

Dorothy's journals, written at this time, reflect the enthusiasm which these new contacts had brought to her life, and she wrote at length on how the Aboriginal 'sense of the sacred' had enlarged her own spirituality. She also continued to write on one of the central issues of our time – that is, how cultures can remain true to their own identity yet live in mutual respect with other, often outwardly contradictory traditions and belief systems.

One day when living in Sydney amidst our Aboriginal neighbours, I found Dorothy almost moved to tears by something she was reading. It was a short piece written by an Aboriginal person and it brought home to Dorothy the real nature of oppression under which so many in the human family live day by day. Yet it also spoke of defiant hope; a hope that would ultimately triumph against all the odds:

> I am black of skin among whites,
> And I am proud,
> Proud of race and proud of skin.
> I am broken and poor,
> Dressing in rags from white man's back,
> But I do not think I am ashamed.
> Spears could not contend with guns and we were
>   mastered,
> But there are things they could not plunder
>   and destroy.
> We were conquered but never subservient,
> We were compelled but never servile.
> Do not think that I cringe:
> I am proud,
> Though humble and poor and without a home . . .
> As was Christ.

Oodgeroo of the Noonuccal tribe

Within a few short weeks of our homecoming from Australia, Dorothy's life on earth had abruptly ended. On the evening before her death she was still busy, by e-mail, on her international campaigning work for a more just creative global order. Her life had touched many people all over the world. She was an immensely gifted and loving person – a companion of God, who walked with tenderness on the path of compassion. She was also, in her own calm way, one of the planet's 'gentle revolutionaries' who never forgot to look at the stars!

We look up and see the stars shining above
and we say, 'They are the
bright suns and around
them are the planets,
possibly with people that
we will never see.'
However, when my
Aboriginal people looked up
at the night sky they didn't
see the stars –
they never saw stars.
They only saw the campfires
of their ancestors on the journey.
The bright stars were the
ancestors who were not long gone:
the dimmer stars were the ancestors
further on the journey.

Eddie Kneebone, Aboriginal elder

Memories

It's the hug,
It's the crazy joke,
It's the warm hand,
It's the fish and chips.

It's the sudden laughter,
It's the silent tears,
It's the high noon,
It's the dark night.

It's the broken bikes,
It's the washing up,
It's the school run,
It's the touch of love.

It's the dog's lick,
It's the loud music,
It's the magic smiles,
It's the stupid dancing.

It's the screaming kids,
It's the loving note,
It's the quick kiss,
It's the great neighbours.

It's the TV switch,
It's the burnt toast,

Finding Hope Again

It's the midnight walk,
It's the lost keys.

It's the local gossip,
It's the easy tenderness,
It's the heart's longing,
It's the morning mist.

It's the hidden pain,
It's the old bracelet,
It's the simple prayer,
It's the long waiting.

It's the truth telling,
It's the searching,
It's the healing,
It's the welcome.

It's the fragility,
It's the strength,
It's the nourishment,
It's the homecoming.

It's the phone,
It's the burst tyre.
It's the washing-up.
It's the silly songs.

It's the wisdom,
It's the energy,
It's the hope,
It's the faith.

Sorrow

It's the intimacy,
It's the parting,
It's the tears,
It's the farewell.

It's life,
It's death,
It's the Spirit
Of blessing.

It's the God
Of surprises,
Met again
On the journey.

Part Two
Enfolded in Love

Nothing speaks but the absence

Dear Ruth and Malcolm

Many thanks for your letter and for all your caring. As a family we have had endless support – it's humbling, wonderful, and incredible all at the same time.

It's now six weeks since Dorothy moved into the wider possibilities of God, and we are all finding life hard to say the least. (That must be the understatement of the year!) I feel so much for the family who are missing Dorothy in hundreds of little ways, as I am.

For my own part, I keep thinking that Dorothy will soon be back home. Back to sharing our crazy jokes; back to telling me how untidy our room is; back to phoning the kids; back to her writing; back to just being herself in our life together on this amazing planet. I even find myself telling Kuti our Labrador that 'Mum will soon be back.' Will these feelings ever go away?

Yesterday I was speaking to one of our neighbours. Dorothy and I had shared in her husband's funeral service a few years back. Maggie was saying to me that, even with the intervening years, she still sometimes expects Alex to come in for his evening meal. And that there are days when she still finds it impossible to believe that he has actually died. Is it similar to an amputation? The limb has been taken away, but you still feel it's part of you.

On that morning of Dorothy's death, a whole part of

us, as a family, just disappeared from our midst. I think it must take months, even years to grasp this truth, and at the moment all our emotions are on a roller-coaster and almost unable to take in anything. Looking back, I have always disliked the expression, 'You'll get over it in time.' If love and affection have been at a deep level, you never actually completely 'get over' the death of someone close. Yet I do believe that you can somehow, in time, integrate this new experience of separation into your ongoing life. I hope I'm right!

The Arabic poet Fadwa Tuqan, in her poem 'A mountainous journey', which is about the situation in Palestine/Israel, has a line that touches me in my guts: 'nothing spoke but the absence'. Fadwa is writing of the situation following the destruction of homes in her native village by the Israeli army, but her words have a much wider resonance. The silences can scream: can shout aloud, as Fadwa knew only too well.

When I awake in the morning, it is the absence of Dorothy's physical presence that speaks louder than any words. As I slowly come to consciousness, with the new day, the first thing that comes into my mind, again and again, is the simple, yet gut-wrenching, fact that Dorothy, who was the life-giving centre of our family, is no longer on earth. Her body lies 200 yards from the house in our peaceful village cemetery. To paraphrase the words of those who went to the tomb on the first Easter morning, 'She is not here.'

At one level we know this. The person we loved is not here. Through the years in my pastoral work, many people have told me how they have tried to 'reach out' to their beloved dead. Perhaps just by constantly speaking to them, telling them what is going on, as if they were in the same room. Or by trying to phone them. Now I more clearly understand these fragile attempts to be in touch with the one who has died. It's a way of coming to terms with a reality that is actually both overwhelming and incomprehensible. I seem to be always calling out to Dorothy – totally believing with one part of my mind (or perhaps with it all) that she is here at home. Present still, in the flesh.

It sure is a strange path to be on – one that you travelled five years ago when Tom was killed in that skiing accident. Your desolation then must have been unimaginable, and yet even at that dark time, you inspired so many of us with your integrity and inner courage. I know you understand our situation now – a fact which means more than you will ever know. Your first note on the day following Dorothy's death is on the mantelpiece and its message says it all – 'There are no words. We are with you in the silence.'

With love and thanks for everything,

Peter

The connecting of hearts

Dear Ian

Since Dorothy's death we have been enfolded in a great wave of love from all round the world. Many of the messages that we have received actually come from individuals and families who are themselves in the midst of pain and suffering. Yet they take time to remember our situation! I think that sorrow, wherever it comes from, links us all, irrespective of our outward circumstances. I tried to put that feeling in these lines:

> Sometimes no farewells
> In that moment of transition
> When death propels us
> Into the wider possibilities of God.
>
> Yet in every place of grief
> That connecting
> Of bewildered hearts –
> Destroying
> The walls of separation,
> Bringing us home
> To one another
> In our fear-filled world.
>
> Shared tears,
> Inviting us

Into a deeper humanity,
A more engaged compassion,
A gentler acceptance of sorrow.

A place
Where wisdom speaks
In the midst of contradiction–
Allowing ancient truths
To illumine
Our fragile times
And
Implode our disenchantments.

Thanks again for caring for this rather bewildered heart.

Peter

And all in the end is harvest

Those who will not slip beneath
the still surface on the well of grief
turning downwards through its black water
to the place we cannot breathe
will never know the source from which we drink,
the secret water, cold and clear;
nor find in the darkness glimmering
the small round coins
thrown by those who wished for something else.

David Whyte

Dear Sue

You were saying that you have not been sleeping well since John's death: it's the same for me. I lie awake for hours and think about these last months and all that has happened to us both following the loss of our soul-mates. There must be thousands of us – out there – in the same situation trying to cope with this well of grief. And in these silent hours I cry my heart out, just as they must do.

About 2 a.m. last night I was walking around and a thought kept coming to me. I wanted to share it with you. I find it hard to express on paper exactly what I was thinking, but maybe it can be put as a question. It goes something like this – Can all this present sorrow actually help me to take more risks for God and live more creatively in the future?

In other words, because of what we are going through following John and Dorothy's deaths, can we learn to live more provisionally, more open to the possibilities of each new day? Do you remember that old Russian proverb which says: 'Each day is a messenger of God.' Having seen the face of death so closely, and become more aware of our own finitude, can we discover a more mature spirituality, which enables us to walk more lightly on this earth?

Or to put it in more theological terms, which I know you would expect me to do – Is this a moment in our lives to receive new graces and fresh insights? David Whyte in his poem, 'Where many rivers meet' is pointing to this kind of experience when he writes of 'the secret water, cold and clear' which one sees only after falling completely into the well of grief. In other words, in the pain we can also discover buried treasure – new openings in life. Which is different from saying that our Creator purposely brings suffering to make us better individuals!

At this point we have options. We can choose to go for retreat and withdrawal because of our losses. I know from my pastoral work that folk do choose this road because anything else is too scary. In a way it's natural. After the death of someone very close, an individual does want 'to withdraw' and we will do that for a time. Yet the question that came to me in the silence of the night suggests another way forward. The way of engagement. A different kind of involvement from that which we had when John and Dorothy were alive, but creative engagement with our world none the less.

Edith Sitwell, who I have always regarded as an extra-ordinary spirit, wrote:

Finding Hope Again

Love is not changed by death
And nothing is lost
And all in the end is harvest.

At a personal level these words link up with this idea that
we can begin, slowly and in our own ways, to take new
risks and to live more provisionally. To believe that our
journeys through sorrow can also give birth to a harvest,
even though we don't know what form it will take in
the years ahead. Can we invite God's Spirit to lead us
into these uncharted waters? As I put it in a prayer which
I wrote not long before Dorothy's death (and knowing
nothing of the tears which would so soon engulf our
family):

Lord of every pilgrim heart
Bless our journeys
On these roads
We never planned to take,
But
Through your surprising wisdom
Discovered we were on.

With Love

Peter

Losing focus

We do not see things as they are
we see things as we are.

The Talmud

Dear Jan and Eric

What is incredibly hard about grief is that you lose
focus. The known markers in your life have all shifted,
and nothing is yet reassembled. It's true what the Talmud
says, 'we see things as we are'. Out there the world goes
on; the seasons come and go; the politicians continue to
remind us that they are our messiahs; neighbours suddenly
lose their jobs; there is no milk in the fridge and so on . . .
but, but, the whole world is out of kilter! Everything is
displaced – revolving and dissolving at the same time.

I am still here in the same place – same house, same
village, same children, same dog, but everything seems
different. The living person who was the reference point
for thoughts, ideas, intimacy, fun, disagreement and daily
support, is no longer on this earth. It's bizarre – and it
must be the same for many others who, in an instant, lose
their partner. I am certain it must take years to refocus,
if you ever do. Perhaps with some folk it takes less time.
Like many of the dimensions operating after a death in the
family, it's unpredictable.

There is a short Breton prayer which talks about sailing in a small boat, while all around the storms are brewing. It goes like this: 'Lord, protect me, my boat is so small and the seas are so high.' Most of the time, I feel I am tumbling about in the ocean – like a cork on a surging wave. It's not very pleasant – in fact it's fairly awful! There is no certainty to the direction – it's not as if you are floating on a raft down a gentle, mountain stream on a hazy summer afternoon, with a bottle of wine. I think I could handle that! It's much more akin to being in small rowing-boat in mid-Atlantic on a January night.

You try to concentrate on what you are doing, and then memories flood in, and before you know it you are in tears once again. Totally vulnerable, and feeling devoid of energy. A good friend says it's like being 'ambushed' and I think that is a totally accurate description. I was in a shop where Dorothy went regularly and was looking for oatcakes when I suddenly caught sight of some marmalade, which we used to joke about together. And right there, surrounded by trolleys and laughing kids and tired grandmothers, I burst into tears – and just wanted to get back to the car park as quickly as possible. Shopping was no longer a priority – in fact, it seemed irrelevant. And the trolleys and the grandmothers belonged to another world. A world far, far distant from my own.

And what I find most frustrating in this loss of focus is that because of it, your life becomes much more self-centred and self-enclosed than you want it to be. I often think of the agony my three children must be going through after losing their mum to whom they were utterly devoted. Yet even as I think of them, and their sorrow, my own distress seems to overwhelm my mind and I can't 'reach out' to them in any meaningful way. In some ways,

I feel that they have not only lost their mum, but also their dad who is immersed in his own sorrow. Is this a typical reaction?

These lines from the Talmud make it abundantly clear that reality is interpreted through our own lens. That is true whether we are in sorrow or not. Yet grief completely distorts, or perhaps more accurately, paralyses, our ability to think objectively about most things. Like the huge waves on a high sea which toss a boat all over the place, bereavement threads its way through our being in such a way that all we can do is survive the moment. To think about the future is almost impossible. How to get through the next hour is the primary concern!

And this sometimes propels me to strange behaviour. The other day I spent twenty minutes searching for Dorothy in a shop – utterly convinced that she was there. It was only as I went outside that I remembered that Dorothy was dead. In this unfocused state we look for our loved ones in shops and in a thousand other places – not because we have gone mad – but simply because we are unable to comprehend reality other than from our own sorrow-filled circumstances.

All I can hope for at this stage is that one day I will become a bit more focused. Can you bear with me till then? You will need lots of stamina, some very crazy jokes, and more than one glass of wine!

A big hug

Peter

Intimacy

Remember, as you read, as you live,
Nothing is ever simple,
Nothing
The more it looks black and white,
The deeper you should dig
To find the grey.
Grey sounds dull, but it is the colour of the mind.

Lynne Reid Banks

Dear Sara,

It's just amazing how many beautiful letters you have
sent me – and they are brimming over with your enthusiasm for living life to the full – come what may. You have
gone through many dark tunnels yourself in recent years,
yet you continue to be an absolutely overflowing well of
affirmation for the likes of me.

I remember as if it was yesterday, when you told
Dorothy and I about your relationship with David and
of your plans to be together. You were so open with us
about your emotional life – and what intimacy meant for
you. Little did we know then what was ahead for you
both. When we heard of David's death we were miles
away, on the other side of the world, and could do practi-
cally nothing to support you, but we walked with you, as

best we could, in our hearts. You wrote to us and said how desperately lonely you felt. You told us that the thought of never being able to see David, or touch him, or have sex with him again was just ripping you apart.

When you wrote that letter to us four years ago, I thought I understood what you meant, but looking back, it was only partial knowledge. I think now, after Dorothy's death, I realize more fully your agony then – a desolation, which still accompanies you. Certainly nothing is black and white – and certainly not in the area of human intimacy, despite what some Christian preachers might tell us! Our emotional and sexual needs have many faces – not all of them attractive! And the death of someone you have been physically intimate with raises another whole raft of questions.

In one of my earlier books called *Waymarks: signposts to discovering God's presence in the world* I wrote these words in the Introduction: 'I don't think I have ever been comfortable with a God who is only located in the churches, and I feel at home with those who in their search for God often stumble and fall. The waymarks about which I have written in these pages spring from a heart which knows inner confusion and rich blessing in equal measure.'

And at the present time, one of the areas where I am stumbling, if not falling, relates to my need for life-giving intimacy in my new situation as a 'single person'. It's certainly a 'grey area' – but the question for both of us, is whether or not there is some kind of glory in the grey. I'm an extremely tactile person, and like you, feel lost without the intimacy which marriage brought to my life. And that is a far wider thing than sex – which is not to down-play good sexual encounters. And added to this fact, is the reality that Dorothy understood, and, I think, valued my contradictory, ever-changing, emotional needs.

In an article which I read recently it was noted that a large number of married men in our society who lose their partner through death, marry within the first year of being bereaved. I am sure that this fairly rapid movement into another marriage is closely bound up with their search for immediate intimacy, for belonging, for an exit from loneliness – even though they may still be in only the first stages of grief themselves. The chances are that their emotions continue to be powerfully bonded with their dead spouse while at the same time their drive for human connection may lead them to the Personal Adverts column in the local newspaper. Of course cynics would say that this search is only to find someone to cook and clean! The fact is that we are made to connect with each other, to be intimate, to enjoy the physical presence of another person.

Out there in the wide world, there are not too many guides for how recently bereaved people deal with all of this. At least not in my limited experience. Do I phone up the chat-lines? Do I make a prayerful commitment not to have any very intimate relationships in future? Do I see this as 'a sign' to be totally celibate and join a religious order (given the realities of our post-modern situation that may not be the best place to try celibacy!)? Do I forget my personal needs and live out a wider compassion – whatever that may mean? Do I just wait patiently on divine guidance? Do I forget I'm human? Do I buy a teddy bear – or do you send me one?

At the moment, I don't feel able to follow any of these routes which may or may not bring human happiness. As many writers on spirituality have said – we all cry out for love, for acceptance, for the touch of another person who values us. And underneath all of that, we long for God. For now, I am confused and often lonely. While I value solitude, I am not comfortable about 'being on my own' for the rest of my life. I know there are many struggles ahead, and I am also aware that I will take several turnings that turn out to be dead-ends. I have been down a few already. Yet I also know that 'grey is the colour of the mind'. Nor is my heart closed, angry or bitter – it's just wounded. And even a wounded heart can occasionally dance. Jean Vanier is right when he says that there is 'a gentleperson of love hidden within each of us':

> The heart, the metaphorical heart, the basis of all relationships, is what is deepest in each one of us. It is my heart that bonds itself to another heart; it leads us out of the restricted belonging, which creates exclusion, to meet and love others just as they are. There is a gentleperson of love hidden within each of us. The heart is the place where we meet others, suffer and rejoice with them. It is the place where we can identify and be in solidarity with them. Whenever we love, we are not alone. The heart is the place of our 'oneness' with others.[3]

Looking forward to your next note – you're great!

Peter

In early spring

Dear Helen and David

You have been through so much since your mum's death, but I really loved the way you were able to cheer me up when I was staying with you in Melton. Without you, I would never have discovered the magical beauties of Rutland Water. Yesterday evening I was walking near the village of Hambledon when suddenly a badger joined me.

Over Rutland Water
A gentle evening light
Making special
An empty road by the woods;
And then ahead,
Within the stillness,
Silently, suddenly
A well-fed badger
On her nightly rounds
Oblivious to
Any companion,
Busy with her busyness,
While
Gifting to my heart
A magical moment
Of pure delight;
Blessing my quiet path

Enfolded in Love

As only
Well-fed badgers can do
On an evening
In early spring.

I hope you'll see this new friend of mine on your next visit
to that beautiful wood by the water, but meantime love to
you both.

Peter

A wider lament

Dear Jenny

The other day you asked me if I was able to put my own grief into a wider context, in terms of the world's suffering. I have found some kind of answer to your question in a wonderful article written by Rowan Williams whose understanding of scripture I admire enormously.

In this article he is reflecting on the Beatitudes in the New Testament. When he comes to the one which says, 'Blessed are those who mourn' Rowan makes the point that when Jesus is speaking as a prophet to Israel about mourning, he is not simply talking about an individual coping with bereavement. I find this insight liberating. Half the time (or maybe the whole time) we worship such a small God – a god of our own devising.

It is very easy to turn these particular words about mourning into an unhelpful platitude. Some of the things we keep saying are empty of real meaning. It's often said – if you feel sad it will turn out all right in the end; or, grief and suffering are good for you; or, God likes you to feel miserable because it makes you a better person.

In his writing, Rowan places mourning against the background of the prophetic tradition in the Bible, where the central issue is the unfaithfulness of the people in respect of what God requires of them. The 'comfort' promised to the mourners is the promise of the renewal of the city, of the Holy place. God is not simply going to console individuals for the past. He will completely rebuild what has been lost and broken – the people, its corporate peace and justice, its wounded integrity. He goes on:

> So learning how to mourn, learning how we speak to each other in the public arena about grief, matters enormously. It is not all that often that we are able when talking about the tragedies and miseries of our society, to speak simply in terms of grief. Listening to many people's experience of our society, what we hear is a deep sense of bereavement and loss. We have been robbed, deprived, diminished – and we have somehow to find words for that grief. We need to revitalize a language of grief.[4]

For my part I recognize that my own grief for Dorothy is linked to this sense of bereavement in our society. I can't mourn only for myself and for my own circumstances when around me there is a huge amount to lament over. This is not to sound either precious or pious! I am not trying to make some huge doctrinal statement! But I live in community. I am a social being. Mine are not the only tears.

In the Bible, some of the prophets are repeatedly exhorting God's people to lament because the city or nation is riven with injustice or corruption – usually both. The prophets rage and grieve over these social sins. Rowan says:

> The greatest words of lament, in the entire Old Testament, are in the Lamentations of Jeremiah, those verses which express an astonishingly deep well of grief

43

over the decay and destruction of God's people and God's holy places – as if God's own sorrow and devastation were finding words in a climax of mourning.[5]

To feel attached to a wider sense of lament is not to lessen my own personal sorrow, but rather to give it greater grounding, depth and movement. It's not something I can easily explain, but I know it is within me. Sometimes as I stand beside Dorothy's grave I think of the many graves which we have seen in Africa with their tiny coffins – holding a young girl or boy who had died of AIDS. I would be a terribly self-enclosed individual if I could not also weep for them, along with weeping for my own loved one.

One part of the Christian message which has always attracted me, even if I have not lived out its implications, is the idea that none of us has a concern that is ours alone. We are sisters and brothers in Christ. When another life is wounded or diminished, I am also broken. It was a truth which Martin Luther King reiterated time and again in his speeches during the early years of the Civil Rights Movement in the States. And it was a truth which permeated the anti-apartheid struggles in South Africa.

Therefore I become less than human if I can only grieve for myself, forgetting the sorrows of others and of the world. I live within a vast global network of tears. Sometimes we forget this aspect of grief in our privatized society in which the autonomous individual is paramount. Yet its recovery is vital if we are to know lasting healing in our sorrow, and to be liberated from an unhealthy self-enclosed grief which can often turn into bitterness and anger.

I like the words attributed to the fourth-century desert father, St Antony: 'Your life and death are with your brother and sister. Gain the life of your brother and sister and you gain God. Lose the friendship of your brother and sister and you lose God.'

As Ever

Peter

Invisible stars

Dear Peter

It's good to be in touch and I hope that you are able to make out some rainbows. We seem connected in many ways. Rita died on the same day as Dorothy and also of a pulmonary embolism, although her last round of chemotherapy had further drained her strength. Never the less, her death, like Dorothy's, was sudden and unexpected. It's been a transforming year!

Having shared our lives together for nigh on forty years, the term 'broken heart' has taken on fresh meaning – a gnawing pain and sense of incompleteness (not just a poetic phrase). Good friends had warned me that sorrow would lead along a rough, unending track. It certainly has done that. Yet alongside that is the love, advice and ongoing support proffered unstintingly by our four children, notwithstanding their own grief.

Throughout the months since Rita's death I have become indebted to a nucleus of trusted confidants who, as needs be, have cheered or consoled, encouraged or exhorted whilst we have talked, walked, e-mailed, dined and enjoyed the theatre, concerts or days out together. Thanks to these brave and forbearing friends I may have been lonesome but certainly not lonely.

Against all expectations my grief has proved an experience to be treasured as well as endured. Like George

Matheson I have learned 'to trace the rainbow through the rain' and glimpsed 'the joy that seekest me through pain'.

I have read poetry and other works outside my normal round; talked to people and in ways beyond my custom. I have gained insights into the problems of living with pain and loss; become more aware of the concerns of those who live alone; and even more convinced of some spiritual existence beyond bodily death. I have experienced the phenomenon of friends and neighbours 'walking by on the other side' and come to accept that Rita's death affected some individuals more greatly than myself.

Yet any gaps left 'where friends fear to tread' have been more than filled by strangers – those 'friends we've not met' – emerging and brightening my life. As Longfellow neatly put it:

> For grief is opportunity
> no less than love itself,
> though in another dress.
> And as the golden sunlight fades away
> the sky is filled with stars,
> invisible by day.[5]

One wise and dear friend wrote, 'I am sorry for you in your loss but my sympathy is tempered by envy – you and Rita enjoyed for over forty years the very best this life can offer.' To which I say 'Amen', very conscious that it is largely the momentum of those last forty years together that has kept me going. I experience no sense of Rita's presence, yet I feel an inner conviction that she shares still in my decisions and actions.

I regret that this is such a lop-sided letter – it's too self-centred! Despite everything, my overriding feeling is one of thankfulness for all the blessings that I have received in these last weeks and in former times. I was born lucky and became more so when I met Rita. Happy memories, and her continuing inspiration, are a wonderful legacy. I have confidence to continue living life to the full as Rita herself did so magnificently. To God be the glory!

Do keep in touch

Mike

A live loving

About four months after Dorothy died, I was visited in Laggan by two close friends, Olive and Bill. They have both been involved, over many years, in walking alongside people with learning disabilities. Bill is a Methodist minister, and Olive was a special needs teacher. After a few happy days together, they set off to drive back to their home in Leicestershire. Then tragedy struck. Just one and half miles from our village a car travelling in the opposite direction crashed into their vehicle. Olive was killed on the spot and Bill was injured. Later, I had the privilege of sharing in Olive's funeral. It was a celebration of a person who witnessed to an engaged Christian faith, which was earthed in her journey with those who have learning disabilities, including her daughter, Helen.

Dear Bill,
   You have been through a terribly difficult time since Olive's death. I am amazed by your inner strength and by the way in which you continue to give support to many others. What keeps you going in these dark days?

Peter

Dear Peter

I believe that when Paul wrote to the Corinthians and indicated the close relationship between faith, hope and love – a trinity of experiences as we journey in life – he offered us some wisdom.

In the aftermath of Olive's death, last July, the response of faith from our shared journey of the last thirty-plus years was amazing, overwhelming at times. I need some time to revisit some of the letters and cards that people sent as the news spread. This process went on for several months.

However, there were some particular notes that touched into my life at the time of their coming and have remained with me. There was a card from a close friend, which simply yet profoundly said, 'There are no words, I am with you in the silence.' Then an encounter with a respected minister and friend, who held my hand as he looked at me with love and said, 'I pray for you every day.' I was touched by love, held by faith, and in this outreaching found glimmers of hope. Hope that life would go on; hope that I would find new ways of being – even in this great void. The void that needs, I think, not to be filled, but sounded!

You may remember on the day of Olive's funeral and thanksgiving service, when we arrived at Queniborough cemetery for the burial, we had to wait some time for people to gather. There was time for greetings and holding, for physical contact with live, loving people. Then the coffin was lowered into the ground. Utter desolation. It took me a long time to go back to the graveside. What am I trying to say? In the 'live loving' there is a tentative hope, which touches into the desolation and the despair. The desolation is not only by the grave, but in other places too

– my bed at night, setting foot again in Scotland with all its memories of the car accident, going shopping on my own, things that steal up on you unexpectedly or which you realize are not going to be easy. Yet in all of these situations, however painful, I have been aware of the 'live loving'. Thank God.

As I have begun again my pastoral ministry among people who knew and loved Olive, there have been, in all sorts of ways, expressions of 'live loving'. This has enabled me to begin to explore the void. Your own love and care have been significant, as has that of many others. I have been fed and watered by local folk, and visited by friends from away – many making special long journeys. I have been greeted by people in the town, mothers of children who come to the playgroup, who have just simply said they are thinking of me and they are sorry. People have let me help them, walk with them, and talk with them. They have thanked me for what I have been able to do, and forgiven me when I have got it wrong. But in these things there are glimpses of the coming Kingdom of God, which gives hope.

One of the widows in my congregation, a marmalade-maker and cake-provider, also joined in a conversation about changing the bed sheets, a task I have physically done for some time, but the frequency was in Olive's control. We concluded that we had to develop a sense of smell and turning the duvet was permitted, and we laughed! In the funeral service for the late Queen Mother there was reference to laughter being a herald for the future – a herald of hope.

So how do I sound the void? Not only in practical matters like shopping for clothes and deciding, what do I need to keep? What are the implications for 'lifestyle' to live without a partner? How do you find the energy for going out on your own? Many questions. I have found myself doing things I would never have done with Olive, or even without her if she were here. That is not to say we didn't have our separate lives in our journey together, but that now I can decide, at tea-time to go to a concert, or to spend the day away, without reference to Olive. This leaves me with a whole mixture of feelings. In *My Fair Lady* he sings, 'I've grown accustomed to her face', and it is a love song.

I could go on for a long time, but I will close now. I am sure there are many issues we can explore further. I guess in the end I continue to be in a vulnerable place, and I pray that on the journey, in the extravagance of God's love, I may continue to find hope. The 'live loving' which surrounds me keeps reawakening not only my own compassion, but also lasting hope in my heart.

Bill

All will be well

Let nothing disturb thee:
Nothing afright thee:
All things passing:
God never changeth.
Patient endurance attaineth to all things:
Who God possesseth in nothing is wanting:
Alone God sufficeth.

Teresa of Avila

Dear Peter

The other day you asked me why I was so fond of Teresa of Avila's prayer. My link with this prayer began when I was visited, some years ago, by an Anglican vicar. She asked me if I could do some work in connection with a person in training for the ministry. We had never met before, but we established an immediate rapport and promised that we would meet each other again.

Some weeks later I had a heart attack and spent quite some time in the coronary care unit of our local hospital. I had a number of 'get well' cards from friends, and amongst them was one from this vicar. On her card were the words of this famous prayer. I pinned it up on a cupboard next to my bed where everyone could see it, and sometimes someone would copy the words down because they found them so meaningful.

I found them exceptionally affirming, as I lay there – indeed they became a kind of talisman for me. If I felt downhearted, frustrated or sad, I would read the prayer over and over again, and it always helped me to get things in perspective.

When I returned home, I kept these words in my handbag, in my Bible – all over the place! I sent the prayer to anyone I knew who was suffering or had problems, feeling that it might bring comfort to them. I even created a 'modern version' of it. Nothing has ever brought me such strength as this prayer: nothing has given me so much hope for the future. Here's my version:

> Do not let anything disturb you
> Nor anything frighten you.
> All things pass: God never changes.
> Patient endurance attains all things.
> Those who possess God in their hearts
> Want for nothing –
> For God alone is sufficient.

And when we were talking I should have told you about Jill who was a special person in my life. The first assignment I had as a church Lay Worker was to visit a woman in her forties who was dying of cancer. She was a delightful person and, as I visited her regularly, we soon became firm friends. She was a truly gracious person whose only real concern at that time was for her teenage daughter, who, having no relatives, stayed with friends whenever Jill spent time in hospital.

We talked about everything under the sun, including

death and dying: she taught me many things, including how to crochet!

One day when she was very weak, I visited her and found her weeping. 'Read to me from the Bible – perhaps that will help,' she requested. 'What do you want me to read?' I asked. 'I don't know,' she said, 'you're the one who's supposed to know what to do and say – it's your job!' We both smiled at this joke, knowing it was far from the truth!

I turned to Romans chapter 8 and read:

We know that all things work together for good to those who love God, who are called according to his purpose. If God is for us, who can be against us? He who gave up his own Son for us all, will he not also give us everything else? Who will separate us from the love of Christ? Will hardship, or distress, or persecution, or famine, or nakedness, or peril, or sword? No, in all these things we are more than conquerors through him who loved us. For I am convinced that neither death nor life, nor angels, nor rulers, nor things present, nor things to come, nor powers, nor height nor depth, nor anything else in all creation, will be able to separate us from the love of God in Christ Jesus our Lord.

As I read these words, I became more and more convinced of their truth. I looked at Jill: her face was radiant. 'Yes, yes,' she said. 'I just know that's right, I know it's true.' Perhaps we were both a little intoxicated by the words we had shared, but it was as if they blazed with the light of the truth of God. Then Jill asked me to write them out in large letters so that she could read them whenever she wanted to.

Whatever happened that afternoon in that hospital ward, it became obvious that it was a crucial turning point for Jill. She caught a vision of what was to be and it restored her hope. When I went the next day, we talked again and reread Paul's words to the small Christian community in Rome. Then when I had finished reading, Jill said, 'I can't wait to get there now, I know it will be wonderful.' The following day she slipped into a coma and died some hours later. I am convinced that Jill died at peace with God, and full of hope!

Let's talk again soon.

Jean

The only option

Dear Peter

We miss Dorothy's inspiration on global issues. I remember when she sent us a little poem you had seen in a leprosy village in India:

> I sought my soul, my soul I could not see;
> I sought my God, but God eluded me;
> I sought my brother – and I found all three.

We try to continue with the campaigns, Amnesty, International Debt etc but just wish that Dorothy was still around to help us!

Ann and Peter

Dear Ann and Peter,

Thanks for your letter. I know how much you are doing to make people more aware of these global concerns. I admire your level of commitment. Your vision for a world in which there is lasting justice for everyone in the human family, and not just for some, is a real gift to many of your friends.

When I think about the extent of human suffering across the globe, I am almost overwhelmed. That goes for lots of others who want to understand the global situation, but find it so complicated and depressing. What keeps hope alive for you in our times?

I know that you have thought long and hard about these questions, and written about them. I am convinced that one path to greater hope is to keep sharing our visions, questions, fears and insights as much as possible. We are part of a growing awareness – a development in human consciousness. The Dalai Lama suggests that despite all the evidence to the contrary, there is in fact a great 'growth in compassion' in this period of human history.

I have always liked that poem which goes:

> Isn't it strange that princes and kings
> And clowns that caper in sawdust rings
> And ordinary folk like you and me
> Are builders for eternity
> And each is given a bag of tools
> An hour glass and a book of rules
> And each must build
> Ere their time has flown
> A stumbling block or a stepping stone.

Meantime take a moment to watch the stars – they have lots to teach us!

Peter

Dear Peter

We did watch the stars last night. It was a beautiful, cool, clear evening. We always try to make ourselves pause. And the longer we pause, the easier it is to remain calm. To let go of everything else and just look up. Despite the stranglehold our pressurized existence can exert on us, we can, at any given moment, actually stop! Yes, just stop. That's sign of hope in itself.

And as we stand still even for a moment, we can gradually reaquaint ourselves with who we actually are as human beings. To be immersed in the present moment with our God. To be amazed again by the miracle that is our earthly life. Sensing the thin dividing line between life and death as our awareness of the eternal begins to affect the way we are. That is what sustains us, even if it's not always easy either to slow down or stop. The rapacious effects of the powerful economic system within which we are submerged for so much of each day can still drag us away from our ultimate truth.

But not for long. We know God is always there in the midst of it all. The conflict comes in realizing that we have to accept our poverty in this world (contrary to the values of the system), and discover a new, extraordinary richness in our surrendered vulnerability. All of this takes courage. Yet people continue to astound us with their compassion and commitment. They are inspiring. Each day they are accepting their inner poverty in this world and through that acceptance doing extraordinary things.

Recently we heard about a young peace activist from Manchester. The other day this women was shot at while acting as a human shield – protecting, with many others, ordinary Palestinian families from Israeli tanks. What makes her go all these miles to be with suffering folk? She described her life back home as 'comfortable'. From this place of comfort she could no longer stand aside and watch other people's suffering from a distance.

It's this kind of solidarity which continues to inspire our work with our local Fair Shares Group. We are only small – a grassroots link to the world from a little Scottish village, yet we carry a lot of hope. For approaching twenty years now we have felt compelled to respond to the pain and impoverishment of our fellow human beings. There is no option. It is simply a reflection of who we are as human beings, placed on this earth which we share with everyone else. It is our awareness of our own poverty before God which ensures that we express, even in a limited way, what is deep within us.

Indeed, we would go so far as to say that it is even a 'celebration' of who we actually are – as we demand, through our Group's activities, that all human beings should be able to join in this great and joyous festival of life as equals. How can we be liberated or joyful while ignoring the agony of others? It's not possible.

Our commitment to the world reminds us that each moment is a precious moment. A moment to act – to become more aware of what's going on around us. Are we not called to try and live as compassionately as possible, with an instinctive and increasing awareness of our neighbours and of the eternal?

In hope and love

Anne and Peter

Belonging

One day, feeling a bit low, I opened the post and among the letters was this poem by a friend who has a home on the peninsula at Otakou in New Zealand. He called the poem 'Belonging' and hoped it would cheer me up. It did.

> On this soft-shining radiant day,
> Grey-silver seas,
> Beneath a massive sky;
> Light elbowing out of the gloom.
> A flirting sun caresses distant hills
> And teases awkward trees.
> Precisely fashioned drops of rain
> Are measured one by one
> On tarmac road.
>
> I walk – it's second-nature now –
> The rim of land and sea;
> Left to my hand
> The zestful quietude of waves;
> A curious seal ups periscope
> Then dives again;
> Click-clacking starlings sigh,
> Acknowledging the crunching surge
> Of Aramoana's power.

Finding Hope Again

Here I belong.
I swim the land
And walk the sea,
I breathe these hills
as they breathe me;
My weightless feet
Touch covenanted soil,
On this soft-shining, radiant winter's day.

Peter Matheson

Part Three
Seeds of Hope

A dimension of the soul

Either we have hope within us
Or we don't.

It is a dimension of the soul, and
Is not particularly dependent
On some observation of the world.

It transcends the world
That is immediately experienced
And is anchored somewhere
Beyond the horizons.

Hope
In the deep and powerful sense
Is not the same as joy
That things are going well
Or willingness to invest in enterprises
That are obviously headed for early success,
But rather the ability to work for something
Because it is good.
Not just because it stands a chance to succeed.

Hope
Is definitely not
The same as optimism.

Finding Hope Again

It is not the conviction
That something will turn out well,
But the certainty
That something makes sense
Regardless of how it turns out.

It is hope
Above all, which gives us the strength to live
And continually try new things.

Vaclav Havel[6]

An unexpected new dawning

These are some lines which I wrote a few months after Dorothy's death, as I was starting to come to terms with the fact that my personal journey in future would be very different from what it had been during the last twenty-eight years. When they were penned, I was at that stage in my movement through grief when I was just starting to realize that new creative energies might emerge out of the shadows of loss. I'm still unsure of what that means, but I try, each day, to be open to them. On the bad days that's not so possible!

> With the
> Beckoning and dawning
> Of another day
> Can the powerful,
> Mysteriously tender
> Presence of death
> Propel me
> To a wider awareness;
> To a calmer
> Acceptance
> Of life's
> Surprising turns?

Finding Hope Again

Can desolation
Invite me to rediscover
The sacred in myself
And in the world?

Through these
Lament-filled days
Can fresh wisdom
Enfold me?

A heart,
Renewed in hope,
Open to wonder,
Breaking these
Imprisoning bonds
Of my endless tears.

Connecting me to
New dimensions
Of compassion,
Of faith,
Of laughter,
Of commitment,
Of forgiveness,
Of healing.
Of surprise,
Of connection,
Of grace . . .

A tentative, unexpected,
New dawning,
Earthed in the blessings
Of all that has been.

Purpose

God has created me
To do some definite service.
He has committed some work to me
Which he has not committed to another.
I have my mission.
I may never know it in this world
But I shall be told it in the next.
I am a link in the chain
A bond of connection
Between persons.
He has not created me for nought
I shall do good.
I shall do his work.
I shall be a preacher of truth
in my own place,
while not intending it,
if I but keep his commandments.
Therefore,
Will I trust him.
Whoever, whatever I am,
I can never be thrown away.
He does nothing in vain.
The Lord knows what he is about.

John Henry Newman

The meaning of things and their purpose,
Is in part now hidden
But shall in the end become clear.
The choice is between
The Mystery and the absurd.
To embrace the Mystery
Is to discover the real.
It is to walk towards the light,
To glimpse the morning star,
To catch sight from time to time
Of what is truly real.
It is no more than a flicker of light
Through the cloud of unknowing,
A fitful ray of light
That is a messenger from the sun
Which is hidden from your gaze.
You see the light but not the sun.
When you set yourself to look more closely,
You will begin to see some sense
In the darkness that surrounds you.
Your eyes will begin to pick out
The shape of things and persons around you.
You will begin to see in them
The presence of the One
Who gives them meaning and purpose,
And that it is He
Who is the explanation of them all.

Basil Hume[7]

Shared journeys

We told our stories, listening to each other
Hearing the journeys of each soul.

We sat in silence,
Entering each one's pain and
Sharing each one's joy.
We heard love's longing
And the lonely reachings-out
For love and affirmation.

We heard of dreams shattered,
And of visions fled,
Of hopes and laughter
Turned stale and dark.
We felt the pain of isolation,
And the bitterness of death.

But in each brave and lonely story
God's gentle life broke through,
And we heard music in the darkness
And smelt flowers in the void.
We felt the budding of creation
In the searching of each soul,
And discerned the beauty of God's hand
In each muddy, twisted path.

And his voice sang in each story:
His life sprang from each death.
Our sharing became one story
Of a simple lonely search
For life and hope and oneness,
In a world which sobs for love.
And we knew that in our sharing
God's voice
With mighty breath
Was saying
Love each other and take each other's hand.

For you are one, though many,
And in each of you I live.
So listen to my story
And share my pain and death.
O, listen to my story
And rise
And live
With me.

Edwina Gateley

Snowdrops and aconites

Full spring is glorious:
the sun dares to be
warm again
in the slowly lengthening days,
as exploding buds
drive far away
the memory of
winter cold.

Already its promise
is advanced in
new growth,
longer days,
greening fields.
and mood changes.

Yet the miracle of spring
came earlier,
when snow still covered the hills
and nights carried frosty air.

It came, unbidden,
when days
were short and
storms swept the valley.

Finding Hope Again

For suddenly,
silently,
gloriously,
utterly unobtrusively,
under bare trees,
close by a full stream,
snowdrops and aconites
announced a dawning.

Signs of awakening
within the
tender mystery
of constant change
and vibrant renewing.

Blossoms of hope–
powerful markers of
resurrection
in confusing times.

What do we ache for?

It doesn't interest me what you do for a living,
I want to know what you ache for,
And if you dare to dream of meeting
    your heart's longing.
It doesn't interest me how old you are,
I want to know if you will risk looking
    like a fool for love,
For your dreams, for the adventure of being alive.
It doesn't interest me what planets are squaring,
    with your moon:
I want to know if you have touched the centre
    of your own sorrow:
If you have ever been opened by life's betrayals
Or have become shrivelled and closed from fear
    of further pain.
I want to know if you can sit with pain,
    mine or your own,
Without moving to hide it, or fade it, or fix it.
I want to know if you can be with joy,
    mine or your own:
If you can dance with wildness
    and let the ecstasy fill you
To the tips of your fingers and toes
Without cautioning us to be careful, be realistic, or
To remember the limitations of being human.

Finding Hope Again

I want to know if you can disappoint another
    to be true to yourself:
If you can hear the accusation of betrayal
    and not betray your own soul:
If you can be faithful and therefore be trustworthy.
I want to know if you can see beauty everyday,
    even when it is not pretty,
And if you can source your own life from it's presence.
I want to know if you can live with failure,
    yours and mine,
And still stand on the edge of the lake
And shout to the silver of the full moon 'Yes'!
It doesn't interest me to know where you live
    or how much money you have,
I want to know if you can get up after the night
    of grief and despair,
Weary and bruised to the bone,
And do what needs to be done for the children.
It doesn't interest me who you know or how
    you came to be here:
I want to know if you will stand in the centre
    of the fire with me
And not shrink back.
It doesn't interest me where or what you have studied:
I want to know what sustains you from the inside
    when all else falls away.
I want to know if you can be alone with yourself,
And if you like the company you keep
In empty moments.

Oriah Mountain Dreamer[8]

Our precious lives

Tell me
   What you plan to do
     With your
      One,
       Wild,
        Precious life?
Mary Oliver

Forgive us
For that narrowness of vision
Which sees only the clouds
And misses the
RAINBOWS.
Women of Guatemala

The only way to eat an elephant is in small pieces.
Desmond Tutu

I am making the right steps,
But not necessarily in the right order.
Eric Morecambe

Finding Hope Again

God has put me on earth
To accomplish a certain number of things.
Right now,
I am so far behind,
I will never die.

Woody Allen

Ancient bearings

The 'Prayer in Six Directions' has sustained indigenous communities in North America through the centuries. In an unhurried way, the seeker after God greets the six directions in prayer.

We turn to the east and face the rising sun. God is praised for the gift of new life, of new days, of new beginnings.

Turning towards the south, thanks are given for those people, events and things which warm our lives and help us to grow and develop.

The sun sets in the west, and so we praise God for sunsets, nights, for the endings in our lives.

As we face the north, we remember the challenges and difficulties in life.

Bending down to touch mother earth, we praise the Creator for the things which sustain our lives.

Finally, as we gaze into the sky, we thank God for hopes and dreams.

Centred in the Creator's universe, we remember the ways in which God is working through our life and walking with us into the future.

Part Four
Bearers of Hope

Sandy

There are some images that stay in the mind forever. Even as I watched Dr Sandy Logie holding the hands of a young African man, dying of Aids, in the middle of the Zambian bush, I knew I would always remember the moment.

Sandy had none of the West's expensive anti-retroviral wonder-drugs, or strong painkillers, to offer the weak, emaciated man sitting under a tree by his dilapidated shack on that sweltering, uncomfortable day. That he was armed only with rehydration salts and vitamins made his tenderness all the more poignant. Patients back in his native Scotland had grown used to his gentle personal style, but it was accentuated that day by shared personal experience, for Sandy was, by then, himself a very ill man, also infected with the HIV virus.

A diabetes consultant from the Scottish Borders, he became infected with HIV in a Zambian hospital some years ago during what he hoped would be the first of a series of placements in Africa. There were several incidents that might have allowed infected blood into his system, during his five-week stay at St Francis's Hospital in Katete, a rural backwater on the Malawi border, but his fate was probably sealed by an accidental prick with an infected needle.

What was so impressive about Sandy – and his wife, Dorothy, who is also a doctor – was his complete lack of self-pity. Right from the time when he first knew he was HIV positive he was determined to focus not on his own situation, but on the plight of millions of Aids sufferers in Africa and elsewhere.

Mary Braid[9]

In this moving tribute to Sandy, Mary Braid was right – there was no self-pity, only concern for others who shared his illness. And it was his courage and compassion, which I tried to highlight when I had the privilege of speaking at his funeral service. As we planned for that event I remember his widow Dorothy saying to me: 'I am sure Sandy would want us to concentrate more on the Aids situation in Africa than on himself.'

Sandy was a good friend who took an enormous risk in 1996 when he became one of the first British doctors to divulge his own HIV status when he 'came out' in an article in the *British Medical Journal*, against the advice of his own health board. Given the prejudice and hysteria around Aids at that time, the board had counselled that as long as Sandy performed non-invasive surgery, no one need know of his condition.

After long discussions with Dorothy and some close friends about the possibility of his 'coming out' to the public, it was, in the end, Sandy's inner integrity which took him down the enormously difficult road of being open about his illness. In the years that followed, as his body became weaker, he never regretted that decision. By making clear to the public, who I believe rightly expect a high degree of honesty from senior medical consultants, that he was suffering from Aids he also did much to ease the disease's social stigma in Britain. And he was well aware that it was a similar kind of stigma which continued to play a huge part in the rampant advance of the virus across Africa.

Sandy's 'coming out' was a personal dilemma, especially for a reserved person who valued privacy. He also felt strongly that being alongside Aids sufferers in Africa was much more important than speaking about his own circumstances, yet when he wrote the article for the *British Medical Journal* it was nothing less than a prophetic statement, imbued with hope:

It was while attending to patients in a rural hospital in Zambia, that I sustained my first needle stick injury, and this was closely followed by two further exposures to blood which was HIV positive. Six weeks after this I had a non-specific pyrexial illness which lasted one week. Back in Britain I tested positive for HIV. We were numbed by this misfortune, but ten days later I had a short break with my wife Dorothy, camping in the Lake District. The great beauty of our surroundings, and the perfect weather had a wonderfully healing effect, helping us to come to terms with our situation.

But why am I writing this? There are several reasons. Firstly, as a means of 'coming out' and no longer trying to conceal my HIV state which has been a big strain. My wife and I have told no lies, but it is increasingly difficult to field queries about my health, my illness, and our future plans. 'When are you going back to Africa?' is a frequent question, and 'So have you retired completely, then?' is another, in slightly disapproving tones, to one who seems relatively young. Secondly, in the light of recent existing advances in treatment for HIV, it is possible that I may survive in a fit state for longer than I had feared, and I would not wish, at some unspecified point in the future, to look back on time spent unprofitably, in effect waiting to fall ill. I would like to continue my work as a physician and will be happier if I can be completely open about my health. Thirdly, some family members and close friends have urged me to declare my state, both for my personal peace of mind and because I can then be in a position to help others less fortunate.

I do not foresee strong adverse publicity, but my wife and I realise that we may have to face some of the prejudice, ignorance, irrational fear and aggression, which other health care workers who are HIV positive have experienced.

Any momentary lapse into self-pity responds to a comparison of my position with that of many patients with Aids, who suffer severe, unsupported illness and die lonely, distressing deaths at less than half my age. During my time in Zambia I was often upset by my therapeutic impotence and inability to provide more than the simplest palliation to terminally ill young men and women, many of whom, especially women, had been cruelly rejected by their families and communities, and even separated from their children. In contrast, I know that I can continue to rely on excellent medical care and all the necessary support to help me through whatever may lie ahead. I do not glibly declare myself fortunate, but truly I have much to be thankful for.[10]

Sandy lived for another five years after writing this article and in that time he and Dorothy were able to revisit Africa, despite his increasing frailty. After making public his condition, he continued to be the gentle, gifted physician he had always been and did much to reduce public ignorance about Aids. During the years of his illness, he and Dorothy spoke and wrote constantly about the Aids pandemic in Africa where already perhaps as many as 20 million have died from the disease.

As his own body became weaker and weaker, Sandy saw with clarity that Aids in sub-Saharan Africa was not only a medical problem but was also having major socio-economic effects. He became more determined than ever to plead with his own government and aid agencies on the issue of international debt which was only bringing further burdens to Aids-stricken countries like Zambia. His passionate vision was in direct contrast to his decaying and pain-filled body, which eventually could no longer carry the ravages of the disease, which paradoxically, had given him such a genuinely prophetic voice.

Through it all, he remained a person of hope. His lack of self-pity was nothing short of inspiring, and Dorothy now continues their international work, despite the sorrow which she carries after Sandy's death. As a tireless campaigner for the provision of really significant Aids prevention and treatment services worldwide, she is herself a courageous and compassionate hope-bearer in our time.

> Now your fight is over
> and the long battle
> with Aids
> a thing of the past.
>
> But it was not your only struggle
> as you tried to tell us

of Africa's suffering
with a prophet's vision.

As in your body
you carried the same wounds
that afflict Africa's children
and their loved ones.

You were no observer
of their sufferings,
but rather, a blood-brother
embraced as their own.

And through your courage
we were changed
to take these kind of risks
which marked your days.

To see the hard path
and not retreat;
to hear the cry of pain
and be involved.

Ani Pachen

Too long have I worried about so many 'things':
And yet, Lord, so few are needed!
May I today, live more simply
– like the bread:
May I today, see more clearly
– like the water:
May I today, be more selfless
– like the Christ.

A prayer from Russia

Ani Pachen Dolma, who died in 2002, was a Tibetan nun, freedom fighter and long-time political prisoner and human-rights activist. She was one of my inspirational people, and radiated that kind of hope which is earthed in almost unbelievable suffering. Her life reminds me of what many people in the world have to endure simply because they speak about the kind of basic human rights we take for granted.

Ani Pachen was born in 1933 in Gonjo in the eastern part of Tibet. Her childhood was a happy one, surrounded by revered lamas and a loving family. By 1956, as a result of the Chinese occupation, tens of thousands of nomads and farmers took to the hills to fight the People's Liberation Army. In Gonjo her father organized the resistance and after his death in 1958, Ani Pachen, then a nun aged twenty-five, was chosen to lead the local freedom fighters.

Four years later she was captured. Her imprisonment was to last for the next twenty-one years. For Ani Pachen these were years of forced labour, insufficient food, and often brutal torture. The conditions under which she was held prisoner were indescribable. After being released she made a brief visit to her childhood home, where she found the people and temples alike devastated by Chinese policies. She knew that she must continue to speak out against these atrocities, and her profound spirituality, which had come to maturity during her years of imprisonment, imbued her with prophetic vision.

She returned to the capital Lhasa and there helped to organize the protests against Chinese rule. When she was warned of her imminent arrest she decided to flee from Tibet. After a dangerous trek through the Himalayas, she eventually arrived in north India where she met with the Dalai Lama and told him her story.

In the final years of her life Ani Pachen continued to tell her story. Whether speaking to officials or visitors stopping in for tea, she spoke for those Tibetans who had been silenced by famine, prisons and fear. The magnitude of her suffering, coupled with her humility and forgiveness, gave her a voice of compelling moral authority. Two decades of imprisonment and torture had destroyed her health, but not her spirit.

In her book *Sorrow Mountain* she reflects with enormous wisdom on the terrible suffering of her Tibetan people. It is impossible to read her writings and be unmoved. As I think of her life which was marked by levels of pain I can't even imagine, I am silenced and grateful. Silenced by the depth of her spirituality and goodness, and grateful that such people are on this earth. In Ani Pachen I see God at work in an amazing way. Her faith tradition was different from mine and my knowledge of Buddhism is limited, yet I know her grace-filled life mirrored the wonderful words of that old Russian prayer. For me she will always be one of the saints – a symbol of courage and hope not just for her own Tibetan people, but for all those who believe that God does not want silence in the face of crushing oppression. Her frail body is gone from earth, but her light still shines – challenging my easy complacency and reminding me of Tibet's continuing suffering.

Peter

One spring afternoon I met with my friend Peter. A more engaged and fully alive person would be hard to find! To meet him is to encounter energy, awareness, wisdom, vulnerability, poetry and laughter all mixed into one. Yet the fact is that Peter is on a tough road – at least that's how many others would describe it.

Not long before our spring meeting, he had just acquired a new wheelchair. A grand one which went well with his new van. Wheelchair and van taken together mean that Peter can travel without help – and being mobile is an essential part of his exceptionally active existence. For a time getting around needed one stick, then it became two, then it became a wheelchair. But he plans ahead, and as his limb-girdle muscular dystrophy gradually weakens his limbs, his ability to prepare for any forthcoming eventuality seems to increase!

Muscular dystrophy has been Peter's constant companion since it was diagnosed more than twenty years ago when he was around thirty. Yet even as a child he felt that there was weakness in his legs and vividly recalls longing to sit down on the ground when queuing with his parents for the circus. This was only one of the many occasions when he became very tired, but not having another body to compare with, he felt it was just normal. It was to be several years before a neurologist confirmed that this tiredness was a symptom of his dystrophy.

But how did he react to this diagnosis? The short answer is – by becoming more active, if that was possible. He did a long cycle tour in France, went skiing, became more committed to his drama group – determined that life was for living. His philosophy was clear – if you wanted to do something, you could do it – even if you were totally drained at the end of it all. At the school where he taught, his colleagues valued his warmth and sensitivity, as did the kids. And in later years when the local education authority had given him a personal assistant, he still insisted on being totally involved, even on the sports field and in the gym. Certainly it became a bit difficult to demonstrate skipping to his class, but he could still show them how to do a forward roll!

One of his present plans is to make a trip to the ancient city of Petra. He knew he could not walk there from a nearby hotel, but wondered if he could go on a horse. That thought has led him to take riding lessons at a stables near his home – all by way of preparation. It is this practical optimism which I find inspiring in Peter and in many other friends with physical disabilities. It seems that the fact of encountering, on a day-to-day basis, what to others would be huge problems brings both determination and energy in equal measure.

The Indian poet Rabindranath Tagore, in his famous book *Gitanjali*, challenges us to be open to all that life offers, and through that openness to live as compassionately as possible. The alternative, he reminds us in his own tender words, is to exist in the shadows, and to lose sight of our true being:

He whom I enclose with my name is weeping in this dungeon. I am ever busy building this wall all around: and as this wall goes up into the sky, day by day I lose sight of my true being in it's dark shadow. I take pride in this great wall and I plaster it with dust and sand lest a least hole should be left in this name: and for all the care I take I lose sight of my true being.[11]

After we had read these words together, Peter said to me: 'In a real sense my own life is a fight against the walls.' I was silent, and thought about that for a long time. Opposite me sat a man in his fifties who was overflowing with compassion for others and our world, who did not seem to have a trace of self-pity, who could look back on his school-teaching career with much satisfaction, who valued his huge circle of friends all over the world, who loved nature and its ever-changing surprises, who cooked the most amazing food and tended his beautiful garden, and who also, if one noticed, was confined to a wheelchair and gradually losing control over his own limbs.

And when I did reply all I could say was, 'You've won that fight long ago.' I was certain of that.

> How is it possible that
> you carry
> so much hope
> in your fragile body?
>
> You who find it hard
> to lift a bundle of
> papers in your arms
> or walk even a few steps.

Bearers of Hope

You who greet me
from a wheelchair
that never seems
to confine you.

It's your spirit
that sings of life,
even as your limbs
journey into weakness.

Uncle Wes

During the last year of Dorothy's life we had the privilege of working with the Wellspring Community in Australia. Although we travelled around the country, our home was in a couple of rooms in the church hall of the Uniting Church in Bidwill Square in the Mount Druitt area of Western Sydney. This is a vast multi-cultural area of mostly public housing which carries many of the markers of urban poverty and powerlessness. Several of our neighbouring families in Bidwill came from the Pacific islands, and we soon began to appreciate various aspects of their culture – not least their incredibly beautiful hymn singing and their mouth-watering roasted pig!

Many other cultures lived in Bidwill, and from our Aboriginal neighbours we gained a fragment of knowledge about their rich and complex traditions which, in coming generations, will help us all to enter more fully into our shared humanity. One of our Aboriginal neighbours, Uncle Wes, was a special person with deep wisdom. Dorothy and I not only saw him as a 'person of hope' for his own community, but as a friend who gave us many insights into our own pilgrimage, and into an understanding of Australia's amazing cultural and social heritage.

One day, Uncle Wes went with us into the Blue Mountains, close to the city. We spent many hours in the bush visiting traditional Aboriginal sites which go back tens of thousands of years. It was a truly humbling experience, enriching our lives in countless ways. As we listened to the stories of his people, we knew that we were in the presence of a Master – even though many might see a person such as Uncle Wes as being on the margins of modern, affluent Australia.

A storyteller, displaced by modernity from his ancestral lands, Uncle Wes is a shining star. Against all the odds, and rooted in a life of poverty and struggle, he speaks 'as one with authority'. And incredible as it may seem, he taught us about that kind of lasting hope which is borne of pain, marginalization and endless economic hardship. And some days after our visit to the Blue Mountains I wrote these lines:

> Bidwill's streets
> mirror its rainbow people;
> not the movers and shakers
> of downtown Sydney
> but the fragile ones
> from many lands;
> those on the edges
> whose stories reflect
> the raw faces
> of urban desolation.
> Like Uncle Wes,
> displaced from his ancestral land
> where his forebears
> have belonged
> for 60,000 years.
> Not one of the powerful,
> but a prophet for our age,
> revealing the contours

of our human journey
into the next millennium.
A storyteller,
whose ancient wisdom
illumines our
fragmented time.
A dreamer,
whose visions enlarge
our capacity for wonder
and remind us
of the mystery of Spirit.
Yet can we hear
his quiet words of life
before our restless greed
brings death to planet earth,
and be transformed
by knowledge
so different from our own?
The choice is ours,
as God made clear
so long ago.

Part Five
Journeys of Hope

Dry bones dancing again

Tiredness grounds me
into a quiet stupor
of the spirit.

I yearn to be inspired,
to be lifted up, set free
beyond the place of deadness.

The struggle goes on,
however,
and you and I, God,
we exist together
with seemingly little communion.

Yet, in the deepest part of me,
I believe in you,
perhaps more strongly than ever.

I am learning of you as a God of silence,
of darkness, deep and strong.

I do not wrestle anymore,
only wait, wait,
for you to bring my dry bones
into dancing once again.[12]

Elizabeth and the Rainbow Man

When I worked at Iona Abbey one of my colleagues was a Canadian, Neil Paynter. Before coming to Iona, Neil cared for folk on the margins (or perhaps at the 'centre' depending on our view of God), whose lives radically transformed his perception of the gospel. Elizabeth and the Rainbow Man affected Neil's life at many levels. Despite all the obvious daily struggles which they faced, they were both 'bearers of hope' who were able to draw forth from Neil particular qualities of his soul. It's not surprising, therefore, that his poetic words about them resonate with love for his two wonderful friends. Neil writes:

I met Elizabeth working in a psychiatric hospital. (It was a place where few of the patients kept track of the days. Either they were unable to – lost in a fog of heavy drugs – or, because the days were all the same, they didn't bother.)

Elizabeth had an amazing and inexhaustible wardrobe and made a point of dressing up extravagantly. She sometimes changed as often as four times a day! And standing, smiling, in a long, flowing, golden gown, a floppy hat – both too big for the short old woman, who looked like a little girl trying on her mother's outfits – long white gloves, bright red lipstick, costume pearls, dangling earrings in the shapes of moons and fishes – she explained proudly: 'I dress this way, darling, because the days are all the same. And if the dirty old days won't change then, by Jesus, I will!'

Through the long afternoons she danced. In the dirty, fold-up dining room. To a music only she could hear. All around her gathered the ghosts of the place – the suicides, the walking dead.

I danced with her sometimes when I was on duty and she taught me new steps. Taught me how to open up and hear the music. Taught me how to dance no matter what.

I met the Rainbow Man working in a night shelter for homeless men. He dressed in bright colours, too – tie-dyed t-shirts, purple hair, pink nail polish. He spoke in colours. It was a depressing, colourless place – dingy, dirty yellow walls, clouds of grey smoke hanging. He was labelled mentally ill, schizophrenic. At one time he had studied fine arts at college, somebody said, and had worked masterfully in oils and acrylics. Now, he worked in Crayola crayon. He drew like a child: dogs and cats and upside-down pink-orange flowers planted in clouds. He got beaten up by the men a lot.

One day he brought a leaf in from a walk he took (he was always taking long walks) and held it up to me and said *to look, to see the light in the leaf pulsing, dancing still.*

I was busy and tired and had forgotten how to see, and said: 'Yeah, it's a maple leaf, so what?' I was oppressed and harried: there was someone buzzing at the door again, paperwork, so many important things to do. 'The light in the leaf,' he said again and danced away in a whirl of wind.

And when I sat down and stopped, I realized that what he meant was: to look and see that energy, that essence, alive in the leaf. He could see it. He was supposed to be disabled but he was able to see the light of God in a leaf and to wonder at it. After weeks of running blind through my life, the Rainbow Man taught me to open my eyes and heart again.

The most significant thing to me about these people, these friends, is that they are living the resurrection experience. They to me are the Christ. Christ in the stranger's guise: walking a road of trials, suffering, enduring crucifixion – maybe daily crucifixion. But, in the end, through their belief in life – through their partnership, connection, union with God – they are able to transform the darkness to light, suffering to joy, death to life.[13]

Letting directions emerge

Vincent, who was originally a teacher and is now in ministry, has gone through a tough time of burn-out. More
recently he has come to a place of peace within himself,
but not by an easy route:

The question of where I have found hope coming out
of suffering in my own life has sent me back over these
recent years, when it's been really tough going. Looking
back, and thinking through has made me recognize just
how much has changed for me in a time that seems so
very short and so very long.

A few years back, I remember a colleague asking
me how I was and I remember saying I felt 'buried' – a
word that kept coming to me in the following months.
At the same time I heard another colleague giving a
sermon. He told us that he was leaving the regular
ministry in order to open up a retreat house in Wales.
The house was going to be advertised under the heading
of 'Time for People'. He spoke about how his ministry
had changed until he came to the point where he felt he
had no time for people, no time just to be.

I remember his talk very vividly, because as I listened
it felt as if steel shutters inside me, that had been holding back what I felt, just buckled away. I knew I had no
time, that I was racing from one activity to another,

always feeling guilty because whatever I was doing – and it was never enough – I felt I should be doing something else. I collapsed inside, and spent the next hour in a room with a friend just crying. I felt on the edge of something, but didn't know what. Later when I went to see my doctor he signed me off work under 'burn-out'.

As I'm sitting here writing this, I can feel again the relief I felt then. But it wasn't complete – he gave me two weeks. In those weeks, I thought, I had to sort myself out, I had to read, get my ideas, my theology, sorted, so I could return to work strengthened. No good. When I went back after the two weeks, he signed me off again, and this time there was no set limit.

Then it all started. I didn't understand what was happening to me at all. I knew I had to get away from people, people in my churches, that is: any one of them, however sympathetic (and I know many of them were), just stood in my mind for these unbearable demands that had buried me. I wouldn't answer the phone, asked that nobody from the churches try to contact me or write to me – and I know they found that hard, but I couldn't be any other way: it was instinctive, survival.

I spent hours just sleeping on the sofa: for weeks I was too exhausted to do anything else. A house we own became empty and needed redecorating, so I took myself off there, to do painting and papering, activities needing no thought, and kept myself out of the way of others. That helped. My doctor asked me to see a counsellor. She helped. She seemed a very strong person, was my strength when I had none. I saw her every week. She told me, at our second meeting, that I wasn't going mad and that when I came through this I too would be strong. I held on to these words.

But it was a long time of fear, uncertainty, confusion, bewilderment, pain – going into what had brought all this about – and anger. I had never been so angry. I was angry at the church, I was angry at God. The church was to me a place of impossible demands, soaking up everything I had to offer, then demanding more. When I'd stopped work I had been working eighty hours a week and thinking I should be working another eighty. I had become numb with overload.

What I felt towards God was fury: I had come into this work from my teaching career, believing it was to be God's direction for me, the direction I was to go in life, and it brought me to this state. The words from the Bible, 'My yoke is easy and my burden is light' were words of bitter irony, and nothing else. I had to get away from God. I wanted absolutely nothing to do with God. My counsellor kept mentioning the desert tradition to me, spoke about my being in the wilderness.

That was helpful later, but in the early stages of my time away 'desert' or 'wilderness' didn't feel the right image: I was out on an ocean, in a very small boat, there was no sight of land and I was being thrown around, day after day, by enormous currents inside me which I simply did not understand. It was the most frightening time in my life, and frightening for my wife, too: neither of us had any idea where it would lead, or where it would end.

Now I'm sitting writing this three years later. I am still in ministry. I've moved to another place, helped to it by understanding people in the church. I've carried on. I look back on all that turmoil and anger and hurt from a place that has such peace in it. I look back on it as a time that was one of burn-out, certainly, but at the same time 'burning away'. I know now I had so much in the way I'd approached life, not only ministry, to leave behind.

As a child, I'd been praised as a perfectionist. That 'perfectionism' was just a huge drain and danger for me. That had to go. It made me look again at attitudes, approaches, words that I had assumed were only ever positives, and see the dangers in them: 'conscientious', 'duty', 'obligation' were some. I had to wait, just that, through the time I was off work. 'No decisions – just wait', said my counsellor. In his book *Grain in Winter*, Donald Eadie, who himself has known what waiting is all about, writes, 'Wait long enough to be reshaped, for the hard times to be good.' That helped. I had to wait, for months, for the momentum of the years to seep away, then I could begin to see, then I could begin 'to be'.

I realized I had been driving myself through life and my particular kind of drivenness had been very destructive. Now, through the same friend who had been with me when my tears started to flow, I was brought into contact with Ignatian ideas – with a God who drew me rather than drove me. I was being tenderly led into a whole new way of looking both at life and at God. Could I really believe it was the things that 'drew me', rather than 'drove' my life, which were of God? The pressure-cooker God who had sat in my soul through my life began to fade away.

It was freeing. It meant I was not dictated to each day, by 'shoulds' and 'oughts'. It was my feelings that mattered. The writer Gerry Hughes speaks of Christians suffering from a 'hardening of the oughteries', and I understood. I found myself looking out on the world with an increased sense of wonder, a sense that had been there from childhood. I remember long periods as a child when I just used to stand and watch, look at things, absorb them – but which had been steadily buried in all of my endless 'doing'.

Slowing down, internally, allowed me to be. 'You've come alive this year, dad,' my son told me. After he told me that, I realized that although I had been around the house a fair amount, I'd actually been on the phone, or in my study, or writing, and only occasionally around, mostly for meals. 'My children only ever see my back disappearing through a door,' said another friend. That echoed.

Having decided I would return to ministry, I went on a solitary retreat. My guide, a Jesuit, mentioned the passage about the friends who lowered the paralysed man through the roof to Jesus, and he left me with the question: 'Who carried you when you were paralysed?' There were four people immediately in my mind, and I know how vital they were to me.

So I've come to where I am now – a place of peace. The peace is to do with acceptance of who I am, and about what I can offer to others. It has to do with valuing that, and with not allowing directions to be imposed on me. I am stronger now. It is to do with listening, staying silent often, being still, letting directions emerge in an unhurried way. It is to do with not worrying and being constantly anxious over trivial things. It is to do, at its root, with a sense of being within a greater being, about which I can use the word God, that is the source of life and of a love that hasn't let me go – though at one time all I wanted to do was hurl it away.

Sorrow unmasked

Your joy is your sorrow unmasked,
and the selfsame well from which your
laughter rises was oftentimes filled with
your tears.
And how else can it be?
The deeper that sorrow carves into your being,
the more joy you can contain.
Is not the cup
that holds your wine
the very cup that was burned
in the potter's oven?
And is not the lute
that soothes your spirit,
the very wood that was hollowed with knives?
When you are joyous,
look deep into your heart;
you shall find it is only that
which has given you sorrow
that is giving you joy.
When you are sorrowful,
look again in your heart;
and you shall see that in truth
you are weeping for that which
has been your delight.
Some of you say,

'Joy is greater than sorrow,'
and others say,
'Nay, sorrow is the greater.'
But I say to you,
they are inseparable.
Together they come,
and when one sits
alone with you at your board,
remember
that the other is asleep
upon your bed.

Kahlil Gibran[14]

Ron's notes

Ron is a Methodist minister in a multi-cultural area in the East End of London – a poet and storyteller, loved by all in his local community, and beyond. Here are some of his stories of hope-filled people and moments.

Clarrisa was a steward in the local congregation;
It was her turn to retire.
We were talking about her replacement.
She noted that all those in office, herself included,
were black.
'We need to reflect the multi-cultural nature of
the congregation,' she said.
'We need a white person in office.'
I wondered how much richer the church
would have been, had she, and others,
received such generosity of spirit
on their arrival.

We danced round the church,
joyful,
abundant in our praise
of the living God.
Black and white together,
worship took wings.

We were talking about the Palestinian/Israeli conflict.
Six-year-old Kiran asked:
'Why do people kill each other?'
I answered:
'They sometimes do it in name of religion.'
A puzzled look:
'But that's not what religion is for:
it's about loving each other.'
'You're right.' I answered,
looking at her innocent face
with tears in my eyes.

It was the evening congregation
gathered around the communion table.
Two young men came in, aged around twelve.
As they walked up the aisle I tensed.
What was up?
I need not have worried.
They asked if they could join us,
Informing us that they were Sikhs.
They said they had come to 'have a look'.

We welcomed them in and
continued our worship
That evening we celebrated the Eucharist and
as we reached the point of
sharing bread and wine,
my inner question –
'Should these young Sikh men join in?'
I thought of my visits to our local Gurwarda –
Always being offered prasad
at the place of the holy book;
always I was fed;

always gently honoured.
Of course they should be offered
Bread and wine.
They courteously declined,
choosing to observe with great dignity
the religious practice of others,
themselves, I hope, gently honoured.

At the end of our road is a residential complex for
   Asian elders
who walk their slow way up and down the street.
At the front of our house is a low garden wall
which women and men from the complex
often use as a resting place,
especially in hot weather.
We started to offer them water,
then conversations began,
names were exchanged, and then gifts
of fruit and flowers were brought to our door.
We began to clean up the wall
and painted it.
Soon it was the most important
part of the garden:
an international meeting place
bathed in the sounds of laughter!

Our son is married to a wise and strong Sikh woman.
They have given us two delightful grandchildren.
Someone suggested to us that it must be a problem
having such a family arrangement.
A problem . . .?
Somehow we don't see it that way.
Kiran a problem?

Simran a problem?
Open, warm, sparkling-eyed, loved children – a problem?
Kiran handles it in a much wiser way.
She recently held up her right hand and said:
'With this hand I'm a Christian.'
Then her left, as she said:
'With this hand I'm a Sikh.'
The wisdom of a six-year-old.
. . . A problem?

Part Six
Hope in the World

A prayer for the 21st century

May the road be free for the journey
May it lead where it promised it would
May the stars that gave ancient bearings
Be seen and be understood
May every aircraft fly safely
May every traveller be found
May sailors crossing the seas
Not hear the cries of the drowned.

May gardens be wild, like jungles
May nature never be tamed
May dangers create of us heroes
May fears always have names
May the mountains stand to remind us
Of what it means to be young
May we be outlived by our daughters
May we be outlived by our sons.

May the bombs rust away in the bunkers
And the doomsday clock be rewound
May the solitary scientists, working,
Remember the holes in the ground
May the knife remain in the holder
May the bullet stay in the gun
May those who live in the shadows
Be seen by those in the sun.

John Marsden

Awakening to our own fragility

A few days after the events in America on 11 September 2001, John Miller, at that time Moderator of the General Assembly of the Church of Scotland, gave this inspiring reflection in St Giles' Cathedral, Edinburgh:

> We meet together here today and mostly we do not know one another. Yet we are not strangers, for we are drawn together by a shared distress. And we who meet here in St Giles' are merely a tiny part of the great company of people throughout the world whose thoughts and prayers are united in sympathy, in grief, in anxiety and hope.
>
> There are citizens of America here today including the Principal Officer from the Consulate General. Some of her fellow citizens here in Scotland have already heard sad news, others fear it will soon arrive. Some have wanted to reach home and have been unable to make travel plans. All are in deep distress at what their country has suffered.
>
> Here, too, are people from Scotland and from other parts of Britain and perhaps from other countries too, some who are already mourners, others who watch and wait for what they fear will be terrible news.
>
> Here, too, are politicians, representatives of elected Government, whose colleagues in similar roles carry

the immense burden of taking appropriate action in response to this week's events.

Here too are representatives of Scotland's communities of faith, from Churches, Synagogues, Mosques and Temples.

And here are ordinary men and women whose lives have been shaken by what has happened, and who wish to spend these minutes together in prayer and reflection.

Through our thoughts and prayers all of us want to give encouragement to those who have suffered, and to support those whose decisions will shape the actions of the coming weeks. On Thursday I was in the Sutherland village of Bettyhill, on the northernmost coast of mainland Scotland. From scattered crofts and farms, people came to sign the Book of Condolence beside the Village Hall. And yesterday morning I was in Dornoch Cathedral with people of all ages, gathered in remembrance and prayer.

The sense of tragedy is universal. There is no hiding from the horror of what has taken place. We cannot erase the image of the aircraft disappearing through the glass walls of the towers, nor the realization that their cargo of precious lives was annihilated in the exploding flames – flames which themselves spelt death for so many.

In William Golding's modern parable of Good and Evil, *The Lord of the Flies*, the horror and cruelty of evil is symbolized by the 'fall through the air of the true wise friend' – whose life was extinguished in that fall. We cannot erase the image of the falling of thousands in the collapse of the entire twin towers. As the story unfolds we shall hear of heroism and tragedy in New York and Washington and in Pittsburgh. And we cannot erase the realization that hundreds of brave, self-sacrificing men and women in emergency services, acting in fulfilment of their own human decency, were enveloped in the terrible cloud of death.

And like the darkest thread running through it all is our knowledge that this unspeakably evil deed was the product of human thought and human will. How we wish we could hide from it all. But we cannot. What happens to faith at a time like this, when an event so terrible happens? Some may find that their faith cannot survive. One of the Holocaust survivors, Elie Wiesel, remembers his first night in Buchenwald, as the flames from the crematoria lit up the sky: 'Never shall I forget that night. Never shall I forget the flames and smoke, which consumed my faith in God for ever.' Who could be surprised if this catastrophe brought some people's faith to an end?

Yet in others this unthinkable disaster will awaken a realization of their own fragility, a recognition of the slender thread by which life hangs. And they may be so confronted by that thought, perhaps as never before, that they will seek out answers to their questions in the realm of faith. There is, in the centre of the Christian faith, a symbol of hope. It is the Cross, which is the signal of the death of Jesus Christ, and also the promise of the resurrection. This central belief of Christian faith presents people with a hope, which helps them to live.

And in addition, they may become aware of that haunting promise which lies within the heart of faith, that God is just: the promise that God will dispense justice for matters which in our earthly life are beyond redress. For what earthly justice can make restoration after destruction such as we have witnessed, or satisfy the longing for restitution, repayment, and for vengeance?

Never have we asked more of our political leaders. For it is on their shoulders that the responsibility bears down. It is their words, which will become military force, and will respond to these deeds. They have said distinctly that This is War. They have the capacity to order the exercise of massive force. But the character of the War is not yet clear, nor has the enemy been identified with any certainty. And we hope and pray that the next steps down the road will not bring death and destruction on other innocents, other civilians going peaceably about their daily lives.

For the vision to which people of faith, people of all faiths and of none, the vision to which we look with longing, is of the Day of Peace. The Prophet Isaiah presents the will of God in these words: 'when the wolf shall dwell with the lamb . . . and they shall not hurt nor destroy in all my holy mountain. For the earth will be full of knowledge of the Lord as the waters cover the sea.'

And we read in Matthew's Gospel the list which Jesus set out of people he called 'blessed', a most surprising list: the people who understand the thoughts of God. They are those who have the spirit of the poor; the meek and those who mourn; those who hunger and thirst to see right prevail, the pure in heart, the merciful and the peacemakers. These are the ones who are citizens of the kingdom of heaven. We pray that they will be at work in the days ahead, as the cities and the citizens rebuild their lives.

'Many are speaking of revenge,' said Frank Griswold, presiding Bishop of the Anglican Episcopal Church in the USA, on Wednesday. 'Never has it been clearer to me than in this moment,' he continued, 'that people of faith, in virtue of the Gospel and the Mission of the Church, are called to be about peace and the transformation of the human heart, beginning with our own.' As the coming weeks drive this tragedy ever deeper into the life of the world, we could set ourselves no better task than that.

'Don't I get a hug?' – a letter from New York

Dear Peter

Following the attack on the World Trade Center in New York on September 11th 2001, I volunteered to man emergency hotlines in the city. Along with millions of others in this state, I'd lived most of my life under the stigma of the 'ugly New Yorker' (we're loud, brash and selfish). The stereotype kept popping into my head again and again that day because as far as I could tell, suffering had dismantled it completely.

As I began to work on the hotline, I felt as if I was seeing the character of my fellow New Yorkers for the first time, and I loved them as never before. I worked beside a woman from Brooklyn who saw survivors of the World Trade Center attacks coming over the bridge covered with ash, and immediately took time off from her job to help out. She never paused to think about the implications of just taking this time away from work – the first priority was to be of some assistance.

Our boss on the telephone lines was a man who was a salesperson. Some of his friends were firemen who were missing, and he was volunteering full time. He worked day after day, with little sleep. Yet he was considerate and gracious with us all and nothing was too much trouble.

But what really touched me was the story of a volunteer named George. George had raised five children, but lost his three sons. One was killed in a car accident at the age of seventeen, the second died of a drug overdose, and the third succumbed to a heart attack. Then on September 11th, one of this two remaining daughters was killed in the collapse of the Twin Towers.

George volunteered right away, and when he heard the news a few days later that his daughter's body had been identified, he still came in to work, just to make sure every else was okay. His fellow volunteers gaped at him, speechless. But George said, 'What's the matter? Don't I get a hug?'

Now I'm sure that this willingness to sacrifice, to try, to persevere against all the odds, becomes a power greater than all the forces of darkness. Looking back on that time in New York, I think of the words of Jesus, 'whoever tries to save his life will lose it, but whoever loses his life for my sake will find it'.

Rick

Molly's risk-taking

Molly Harvey, a grandmother in Glasgow, was arrested in a peace demonstration organized by many different groups, including the churches, at Faslane, the nuclear submarine base on the river Clyde.

My decision to break the law
was not taken lightly –
but for two main reasons.
I felt that I would
be failing my children
and grandchildren if
I did not take action
against first-strike
nuclear weapons
on our doorstep.
And
I felt I would be failing
the people living in poverty
with whom I work in partnership,
if I did not speak out
against the obscenity
of the expenditure
on these weapons
of mass destruction

of the equivalent
of £30,000 a day
since the
birth of Christ.

Elis and his mates

'How can we determine the hour of dawn,
when the night ends and the day begins?'
asked the Teacher.
'When from a distance you can distinguish
between a dog and a sheep,'
suggested one of the students.
'No,' was the answer.
'Is it when one can distinguish between
a fig tree and a grapevine?'
asked a second student.
'No.'
'Please tell us the answer then.'
'It is, then,' said the wise Teacher,
'when you can look in the face of a
human being and you have enough
light to recognize in him or her
your brother or sister. Up till then
it is night and darkness is still
with us.'

A Hasidic tale

We grow weary of hearing how bad race relations are in
various places. They may be, but by a long way it's not the
whole story, and it would be great to hear more about folk

of different religious and cultural backgrounds who live in harmony – learning from one another.

Which brings us to Elis Suferi who has become something of a hero at All Saints secondary school on the eastern edge of Glasgow. The thirteen-year-old Macedonian asylum seeker is a fantastic footballer, and since his arrival in the city has done wonders for the school team – in fact he's transformed it, and taken it, into the final of the Glasgow schools championship. 'They are very happy with me,' he says shyly. 'And I am very happy here.'

Elis joined the school after arriving in the UK on his own. He has not seen his mother since she put him on a bus in Macedonia, and is one of sixty-two young people from twenty-four countries at All Saints. The school was one of the first to take the children of asylum seekers when Glasgow signed up for the government's refugee dispersal programme. All Saints may sit in a landscape of outward deprivation – decaying housing estates and empty industrial sites, but inside it's a special place which is living out that truth contained in the old Hasidic tale. For me it's a place of celebration.

The headteacher is the first to say that this influx of different nationalities has not only transformed the football team, but the whole school: 'It has been an outstanding success from many points of view. It has made the school a better place. Many of our children are disadvantaged in life, and into their community come people who have suffered even more, and they have brought with them culture and experiences that are benefiting the whole area. What they bring rubs off on the Glasgow youngsters. They see what value these young people put on education and it is starting to show itself up in performance.'

A multi-lingual centre has been set up in the school

staffed by four new teachers, and local children are being encouraged in a variety of ways to reach out to their new classmates. Teachers said that they could not think of a single incident of conflict between the incomers and the area's own youngsters.

In the playground, Elis's teammates crowded around him, happy to sing the praises of their star midfielder. 'Elis is a great player and he's really friendly,' said his classmate Alan. 'He's just like anyone. He's one of us.'

Generations ago, Hasidic scholars reminded us that the dawn has come to our lives when we see in the stranger our own sister or brother. Until then we are in darkness. So when we hear in the news of mistrust and hatred between communities who carry different cultural roots, we might just pause and remember Elis and his mates on the football pitch in the East End of Glasgow. They are stars in more ways than one!

A contemporary tale

Once upon a time there
was a researcher who
made an incredibly important
scientific discovery.

She discovered the
principle of compassion
and happiness.

Many high-powered committees
met day after day in order
to turn this important
discovery into a
commercial product.

The committee struggled
with the issue, but any attempt
to turn the newly found principle
into a product
eluded them.

A more high-powered
committee took over
the work.

'What good are compassion and
happiness, if at the end of the day,
they don't bring a healthy financial return?'
said one of the group.
'What good is a healthy financial return
if it does not bring compassion and happiness?'
replied the researcher.

A garden of hope

One of the great books of the twentieth century was Nelson Mandela's autobiography, *Long Walk to Freedom*. Archbishop Desmond Tutu wrote of the book:

> The authentic voice of Mandela shines through these pages, humane, dignified and magnificently unembittered. Justice, freedom, goodness and love have prevailed spectacularly in South Africa and one man has embodied that struggle and its vindication. This is his story and the story of that struggle and a people's victory. It will help us never to forget, lest we in our turn repeat the ghastliness of apartheid.[15]

There is little doubt that Mandela's story is one of the most extraordinary political tales of the last century. Emotive, compelling and uplifting, the book is the exhilarating story of an epic life; a story of hardship, resilience and ultimate triumph told with clarity, eloquence and humility. It bears testimony to the power of the human spirit to transcend the structures of a diabolical system. All over the world, millions were moved to tears on the day when Mandela walked into freedom after twenty-seven years in prison. It was a turning point in human history.

Mandela's book continues to touch my own path at many levels. As I reread it, what becomes clear, through his candour and sensitivity, is that no matter how tough the situation in South Africa, he remained a bearer of hope – and acted out that hope in very simple, but concrete ways. He was able to turn his long years of imprisonment into a marvellously creative time – constantly reaching out to others without bitterness. The relationship he had with the prison officers is in itself a remarkable story.

From the extremely harsh conditions of the prison on Robben Island, Mandela was eventually transferred to Pollsmoor prison. His new home had some consolations. The food was far superior, and a fairly wide range of news-papers and magazines was permitted. There was also a radio, but it received only local stations and not the BBC World Service, which was what he really wanted. Prisoners were also allowed out on a terrace for several hours each day, except between twelve and two when the warders had their lunch.

On Robben Island he had been forced to do his daily exercises in his cramped cell, but at Pollsmooor he was able to follow his usual regime of stationary running, skipping, sit-ups and fingertip press-ups in a larger space. This early morning regime did have problems, however, as he was an early riser and soon began to disturb his comrades who needed more sleep! They also found this regular, disciplined work-out a bit over the top.

It was while in Pollsmooor that Nelson Mandela devel-oped his amazing garden. It is hard to imagine a more powerful 'sign of hope' in such a situation. His description of the garden is short, yet it has the ring of a prophetic statement, and it opens a window into the soul of one of the greatest leaders of our time. It is truly a song of hope:

The Bible tells us that gardens preceded gardeners, but that was not the case at Pollsmoor, where I cultivated a garden that became one of my happiest diversions. It was my way of escaping from the monolithic-concrete world that surrounded us. Within a few weeks of surveying all the empty space we had on the building's roof and how it was bathed in sun the whole day, I decided to start a garden and received permission to do so from the commanding officer. I requested that the prison service supply me with sixteen forty-four-gallon oil drums that they sliced in half for me. The authorities then filled each half with rich, moist soil, creating in effect thirty-two giant flowerpots.

I grew onions, aubergines, cabbage, cauliflower, beans, spinach, carrots, cucumbers, broccoli, beetroot, lettuce, tomatoes, peppers, strawberries, and much more. At its height, I had a small farm with nearly nine hundred plants – a grand garden!

Some of the seeds I purchased and some – for example, broccoli and carrots – were given to me by the commanding officer, Brigadier Munro, who was particularly fond of these vegetables. Warders also gave me seeds of vegetables they liked, and I was supplied with excellent manure to use as fertilizer.

Each morning, I put on a straw hat and rough gloves and worked in the garden for two hours. Every Sunday I would supply vegetables to the kitchen so that they could cook a special meal for the common-law prisoners. I also gave quite a lot of my harvest to the warders, who used to bring satchels to take away their fresh vegetables.[16]

No outcasts in the circle!

The moment I read this reflection by Alex Logan, who is a curate in the Anglican Church, I was attracted by the huge sense of hope of which it spoke. What she found in the 'common cathedral' in Boston was a million miles from some superficial, packaged optimism. It was an expression of authentic hope – something that must surely bring joy to our truth-telling God!

Five years ago I read an article about a church which the homeless people of Boston called 'common cathedral' – and a priest called Debbie who began her ministry 'telling stories' with homeless people and asking them to tell her about God. Six years on, in a public park, in the middle of an American city, this unique church community has become a sacred space and a sign of hope for a congregation, which has to be seen to be believed!

Debbie's vision for this church is encapsulated in these words: 'We always want to make our circle wider and wider. We want to include people too frightened, too high, too angry, too lost to come closer: to make room for people who come to us for clothing, for food. To welcome people who drink, who talk while others pray. How can we make our circle wide enough to intervene and protect people, who, if they follow their own path, will die of alcohol and drug abuse?'

I felt drawn in by that too. It sounded like the Gospel. I heard the voice of someone who loved this community of homeless, searching people – whom she describes as my 'dearest treasures' – and who loved God more than her own need for power or affirmation – and it made me wonder if love could be enough after all.

I was drawn back into the church myself by the promises of a God who said that this kind of love could turn mess and shame into a life worth living, and I have returned time and time again to places where Christ comes face to face with brokenness and despair. Over a period of ten years I have followed him down the rabbit hole to 'sink' estates on the outskirts of cities where whole communities are quietly forgotten, and into Bed and Breakfast hotels where people feed their children on jam sandwiches and walk round discarded needles on the stairs.

I have sat on toilet floors with people having alcoholic fits, and seen what 'care' systems do to the young people they are meant to protect. I have been constantly drawn to the edges, to places at the end of the line, to see if God is where he says he is.

In the process I noticed two things about how the church responds to God's 'bias to the poor'. We know how to 'care' for people by providing money, food and shelter but rarely do we draw the same people into Christian communities and make them our teachers. The second thing I knew, working in the voluntary sector as a resettlement worker was that Christian 'projects' for those recovering from addictions are often based on 'rules' and 'systems' which rob people of their individuality and set them up to fail. Paulo Freire insisted that true liberation is about dialogue which is the opposite of being silenced. He wrote: 'Human existence cannot be silent, nor can it be nourished by false words, but only by true words through which men and women transform the world.'

A church in which homeless and housed people worshipped and prayed together seemed to me to have everything to do with what Friere was talking about, so I went to Boston to find out if 'common cathedral' was real. 'Common cathedral' had become a mythical quest for me, a search for some kind of holy grail. Yet as I watched the preparation for worship on that first Sunday there was nothing mystical about it. I watched as a wooden altar was wheeled across Tremont Street, and positioned in front of Brewer Fountain, a place where many of Boston's homeless community gather to talk, sleep and sometimes die, on the wooden benches.

I kept watching as the Gospel was preached and people were invited to come into the circle to speak, pray, cry and 'do business' with God among the pigeons, the skateboarders and the tourists. People who are mentally ill, addicted, lonely or just puzzled, regularly stop to see what is going on and some decide to stay. I began to understand why this community has never moved away from the fundamental basis that it is the poor who teach the rest of us about who God is, not because poverty is redeeming, but because they have none of the barriers to knowing him that the rest of us hide behind.

It is this understanding of who God is which leads to a church community committed to truth-telling, openness and vulnerability. This church acknowledges human brokenness whether we sleep in a doorway or a penthouse flat. Christ is the source of a commitment to being wholeheartedly 'with' people who are 'outside' physically, emotionally or spiritually. It is this commitment which has enabled 'common cathedral' to retain its identity as a church on the margins, a sacred space at the end of the line.

There is some serious 'kingdom' subversion going on in this church! Those who have been silenced come forward and speak their truth. Those who have felt condemned and worthless find grace and forgiveness. The vulnerability through which we were labelled creates instead a bridge to the other person. The space – the circle – is not threatening, not hierarchical. And in this place of sacredness, every contribution is received with gentleness and respect, with clapping, murmuring and shouts of encouragement from the gathered community. I have never been in a church community which feels so open-handed, or so open to God's grace.

In the aftermath of the events of 11 September 2001, which happened while I was in Boston, I realized that it is communities like 'common cathedral' which will teach the rest of us the price, and the gift, of vulnerability – because they have been living it for years. The openness to whatever might happen doesn't always feel comfortable but it does feel real. I could hear my own language changing in response to it. That is one of the things that 'common cathedral' does – even just for a passing friend.

After the service Eddie, a member of 'common cathedral', asked me why I had come. When I told him he grinned at me and said, 'Welcome home.' Now I do believe that God really is at the end of the line, subverting our history with a miracle.[17]

Defiant hope

My heart is moved by all I cannot save:
so much has been destroyed.
I have to cast my lot with those
who, age after age, perversely,
with no extraordinary power
reconstitute the world.

Adrienne Rich[18]

Between one and two million of our sisters and brothers are living a fragile existence in the jungles of Burma, with some 130,000 forced to live in refugee camps along the Thailand–Burma border. They are there because they are fleeing the soldiers of the Burmese military junta, which came to power forty years ago.

It is estimated that these soldiers are killing around ten thousand people each year, although there are no accurate figures. In the last ten years, the army has conscripted about 3 million people, including women and children to porter for them. The brutalization and yet defiant hope of these children can be seen in their extraordinary crayon drawings.

In one, a woman is forced to watch as her baby, lying naked in a giant wooden pestle, is about to be crushed by a rice pounder. Around this horrific scene, troops plunder or kill livestock and murder a villager. The anguish on the face of the mother and the cold misery on the face of the soldier holding her arrest the viewer. Another picture brings home the reality of the political situation for thousands of Burmese people. Refugees are making their way over a river to Thailand, only to be greeted by threatening, armed soldiers. They have no choice but to keep moving forward because the temporary camp they came from has been torched: it blazes in the hills behind them.

The pictures were drawn by young people between eight and fourteen living in a refugee camp north-west of Bangkok. They poignantly and graphically define their circumstances of suffering in which families are constantly hunted down and slaughtered mercilessly as they flee from their jungle villages.

James Mawdsley, who himself spent more than a year in a Burmese prison, commenting on the pictures, said:

As Christians we know that God is everywhere and in everything and for that reason there is always reason to hope. In this place of such massive human misery, the basis for this hope is the Burmese people themselves – their great resilience, humility and courage. Despite all that these children have been through and the unspeakable brutality they have endured, they appear still to be serene and happy young people. I cannot tell what lies beneath the surface and there must be much, but superficially they are the same as children all over the world. We watch them playing; they laugh, they run, they wonder, they giggle.

Part of the explanation for this apparent normality is that in the refugee camp they have had some months of relative security to recover, but there is a deeper reason and one that we can celebrate. It is the way God has made us, and children especially. Despite their past, these children are able to live in and enjoy the present. They are not overwhelmed by worries about the future. The evil that has been inflicted upon them has not corrupted them, and their spirits can celebrate life.[19]

Most of us will never experience this level of brutality in our lives, but we can take strength from this energized and defiant hope which these Burmese children live out, even in a refugee camp. We walk in solidarity with them. In their apparent powerlessness, and living on the margins of our globalized world, they may just be, in the purposes of God, the very ones who are reconstituting it and bringing us healing.

Our grief is not a cry for war

On 11 September 2001, Craig Scott Amundson was working in the Pentagon in Washington. That morning, along with many others, he was killed in the terrorist attack on the building. His widow, Amber, later led a 'Walk For Healing and Peace' from Washington to New York. One of the banners carried during the walk had on it the words, 'Our grief is not a cry for war.' Amber also wrote a public letter to the American President – a prophetic letter, resonant with hope:

Dear President Bush

I am a single 28-year-old mother of two small children. The reason I am a single mother is because my husband was murdered on September 11th while working under your direction. My husband Craig Amundson, was an active-duty multimedia illustrator for your Deputy Chief of Staff Personnel Command, who was also killed.

I am not doing well. I am hurt that the United States is moving forward in such a violent manner. I do not hold you responsible for my husband's death, but I do believe you have a responsibility to listen to me and to hear my pain.

I do not like unnecessary death. I do not want anyone to use my husband's death to perpetuate violence.

So, Mr President, when you say that vengeance is

needed so that the victims of September 11th do not die in vain, could you please excuse Craig Amundson from your list of victims used to justify the attacks?

I do not want my children to grow up thinking that the reason so many people died following the September 11th attacks was because of their father's death. I want to show them a world where we love and not hate, where we forgive and not seek out vengeance.

Please, Mr President, help me honour my husband. He drove to the Pentagon every morning with a 'Visualize World Peace' bumper sticker on his car. He raised our children to understand humanity and not to fight to get what you want. When we buried my husband, an American flag was over his coffin. My children believe the American flag represents their dad.

Please let that representation be one of love, peace, and forgiveness. I am begging you, for the sake of humanity and my children, to stop killing. Please find a non-violent way to bring justice to the world.

Sincerely

Amber Amundson

Marks of love

There is precious little acceptance in our society
of the changes in our bodies,
brought about by sacrifice,
by the giving of life to others.
People want us to look unscathed, unscarred,
without the sagging in our breasts,
the stretch marks in our stomach,
the lines of strain and struggle.
We are to look ageless, timeless,
the image of the lithe and slender.
Where is the place for the beauty
derived from love
and developed through sacrifice?
Where are the people who will celebrate
the signs of someone who has given themselves
to others
through touch and tears and love
unnumbered times?
Who of you will join me
in the risk of being worn out,
of being wrinkled,
of being thrown away?
We are not fools,
who give what we cannot keep
to gain what we cannot lose.

Angie Andrews

Part Seven
Christ's Hope

The gentle friend

Christ is our friend,
The one who is gentle,
Who offers himself,
Who loves,
Who forgives,
Who sustains,
Who regenerates us,
Who sets us free.
So love with enthusiasm
The one who loves you
Even to the point of death
And do not look for
Anything else,
But his love.
In this way,
The Lord will be in the midst
Of you
And will renew you,
In his love.
Live in trust,
And entrust your whole life
To him.
He will be worthy of
Your trust,

Finding Hope Again

And will guide you
Towards the joy
Which is beyond
All understanding
And which
Never disappears.

*Patriarch Bartholomew
of Constantinople*[20]

Returning home

I believe that behind the mist the sun waits.
I believe that beyond the dark night it is raining stars.
I believe that this lost ship will reach port.
I believe I will not be robbed of hope.

From Chile[21]

If it were possible to fathom the human heart, what would we find there? Might we not discover that in our depths there is always this longing for 'a presence'? Brother Roger of the Taizé Community often talks of this heart-longing as 'the silent desire for communion'.

In the days following Dorothy's death, I walked for hours over the mountain paths near our cottage in Laggan in the valley of the fast-flowing Spey. Often my mind was blank. I was not able to focus on anything. Sometimes I would speak to Kuti, our faithful black labrador, who was by my side or busy discovering some magical smells beneath the pines. For the most part I felt utterly lost; the road ahead appeared totally uncertain. I just seemed overwhelmed by events in my life. As a friend said, 'It's like a wall of desolation in front of you.'

Then, as if from nowhere, would come this 'silent desire' welling up within me. A powerful longing which seemed to operate at many levels in my being; it was there in my head, in my heart, in my guts. It brought me to tears – this deep longing for communion with what many writers have called 'the Ground of our Being'. An almost unconscious 'reaching out' for that place of ultimate meaning.

In the Gospel, the story of the Prodigal Son has several layers of meaning. Yet running through the heart of this particular narrative is the theme of 'homecoming'. It is about the possibility of coming back to where you belong – despite many wanderings and mistakes. It's like running up a familiar road near home into the welcoming arms of a person who appears to have limitless love for you – even though they know you well, and are fully aware of what you have been up to in London, or wherever! And sometimes on these lonely Highland moors, in my own grief-stricken wanderings, this story of the younger son coming back to his farm after being in the fast-lane, kept filtering into my numb mind. Dorothy, who I loved so much, was gone from this earth, but were there other arms to enfold me in an even greater love?

And as I thought about this, I also remembered many of the great people whom I have met along the road who have never experienced a deep human love. I was thinking of Jenny who was lifted, like a suitcase, from one council home to another during the first eleven years of her life. And then in her early teenage years she knew what it meant to have the body she was never especially proud of, abused time and again.

And then that longing of the soul returned. Not only for myself in my sorrow, but also for Jenny now trying to come to terms with her wounded youth, and for others who I knew were weighed down by tears. Could we all return home? Was it possible to discover, like that younger son all those years ago, that a lost ship would find port?

I am still on that journey, but there are moments when I

know, in that deep place of knowing, that the sun does wait beyond the dark night. In other words – that God is. In that place of silent communion I encounter One who understands me so much better than I understand myself. And my tears are not disconnected from this awareness. On the contrary, they are part and parcel of this returning. Or to be more accurate, they are at its core.

Centuries ago, my Celtic forebears seemed to know a lot more than I do about this 'homecoming' – finding that place of silent communion – when they shared these words with one another:

> God be with thee in every pass,
> Jesus be with thee on every hill,
> Spirit be with thee in every stream,
> Headland and ridge and moor.
>
> Each sea and land, each path and meadow,
> Each lying down, each rising up,
> In the trough of the waves,
> In the crest of the billows,
> Each step of the journey thou goest.
>
> *Gaelic traditional*[22]

Illumining even the shadows

Are there realities which make life beautiful and of which it can be said that they bring a kind of fulfilment, and inner joy? Yes, there are. And one of these realities bears the name of trust.

Do we realize that what is best in each of us is built up through simple trusting? Even a child can do it.

But every age has its troubles – being abandoned by others, seeing those we love die. And for many people today the future is so uncertain that they lose courage. How then can we leave worry behind?

The source of a confident trust is in God who is love. God's love is forgiveness; it is inner light. A Christian thinker of the seventh century, Saint Isaac of Nineveh, wrote, 'All God can do is give his love.'

This trust that comes from the depths does not lead us to flee responsibilities, but rather to remain in places where human societies are in turmoil or out of joint. It enables us to take risks, to keep going forward even in the face of sorrow and failures.

And we are amazed to find that this trust makes us able to love with a selfless love, one which is not at all possessive.

It is a trust which illumines even the shadows of our souls.

Brother Roger[23]

Life – a fragment of death

Our life is a fragment, naturally, a fragment of death. The life which is reborn to a living hope also remains a fragment. But it now becomes a fragment of the coming beauty of the kingdom of God. Death is not the end of life in the Spirit. This life will be fulfilled in the new creation. Thus with the fragmentary life in the Spirit there is already beginning now the eternal life in the midst of a life which is leading to death. The Christian lifestyle is born out of this certainty. In living community with the Messiah Jesus, the small, incomplete human life becomes the messianic sign of the coming fulfilment of history.

Jürgen Moltmann[24]

On the evening of Dorothy's death her body was taken to our local hospital in Inverness. The Highland roads were dark and quiet as a friend and I followed the small van which held her mortal remains. From the moment we drove out of our village I felt I was drowning in tears. And yet on that dreadful evening as I tried to take in what was happening, the thought that kept coming back time and time again was what a truly good person Dorothy had been when she was on earth. And would her goodness live on?

She would never have considered herself 'good' in any

kind of pious way. She was a strong, highly articulate person who was never afraid to question the established order when it held within it injustice, superficial arrogance or abusive superiority. For many people it was her total integrity which shone like a beacon in a world of easy options. Dorothy never opted for quick popularity, yet she knew what it was to laugh, to love tenderly and not to take herself too seriously! Her goodness was innate, and her calm serenity reassured countless people through the years.

In the months following Dorothy's death, I tried to reread some things which we had both found enlarged our spiritual life. Jürgen Moltmann's *The Open Church* was a book we valued. This particular passage which I rediscovered fills me with hope. I find solace in his idea of life being 'a fragment of death' and that this death can never be the end of life in the Spirit. And it is this 'life in the Spirit' which begins in the here and now – within the many levels of everyday living, not somewhere else! And if this is true, as I believe it is, life and death are together enfolded in this great continuum of God's energy and mystery.

A couple of years ago, Dorothy was in the midst of writing an article about human sexuality when she quietly said to me: 'For me at least, our sexuality moves within a vast frame in which all our very differing sexualities are held. In our lifetime we may be at many places in this framework. We hold in ourselves such complex drives and needs, and yet they are all operating within this much wider spectrum.' It was a view-point which enabled her to understand the mystifying maze which contains our sexual and emotional lives in a wonderfully tender way!

This perception of the 'wider frame' holding many

differences within it, is true of our life and death in God. That is why we can accept that life itself is a kind of fore-taste of what is yet to come – a fragment in the here and now of a much more encompassing reality. Held in God's Spirit there is no essential disconnection between life and death: in both states we are 'enfolded' in the heart of God. And because this is true, at the moment of death, as the physical body dissolves, breaks up, there is this profound regeneration of the spirit.

Living on the island of Iona, off the west coast of Scotland, I became tremendously aware that the Celtic church lived in this conviction – that life and death were different parts of the one reality. This is reflected in some of the prayers which have come down to us through the centuries. My Christian forebears walked gently and in friendship with those who had gone on before them. They did not need the term 'the communion of saints', for they knew intuitively that everyday living was blessed, perme-ated and guided by those who were now in heaven. Yet this was never understood in a morbid way or because they had an obsession with death. They walked with it lightly for the simple reason that it was an energizing force for life.

This life-giving companionship with the dead had at its core a joy and a strongly rooted optimism which is reflected in these warm, almost sensuous, poetic words:

> May the peace of God,
> The peace of Columba kindly,
> The peace of Mary mild, the loving,
> Walk with you this day and always.[25]

Today in our modern societies we have largely forgotten this underlying connectedness in God. In our loss of a sense of mystery we have also lost to our imagination the truth that life and death are held in a seamless entity. Yet, even today, other cultures can help us to relearn this basic truth if we are prepared to listen to them with sensitivity and humility, recognizing our own spiritual poverty.

India has taught me hundreds of lessons, and being there for many years was a lasting privilege. Living in that extraordinary, ancient culture meant that Dorothy and I were on a fast learning curve almost every day! Once, after we had celebrated Holy Communion on a Sunday evening in St Andrew's Church in Madras in South India, a family came over to our home to visit us. Just as they were about to leave, their younger son, aged about twenty-seven, had a sudden heart attack and died. In the tears that followed, the mother of the family said something to us that I will never forget. Her words were: 'Are we not all so blessed and grateful to God that just before he took this attack Ajit had been in God's house, taking the body and blood of Jesus?'

As a Western person I was seeing this sudden and traumatic death as a disconnected experience. A perception that was very different from that of the grief-stricken woman of faith and wisdom in Madras. That mother, even in the face of this shockingly rapid death of her son, saw at once the link between his death and his sharing of the body of Christ an hour earlier. The two events were in her understanding of Christian mystery threaded together. In that moment of her own personal agony she was immediately able to recognize a vast canvas of meaning rooted in God's eternal purpose. Or to put it another way, Ajit had only a short distance to travel into the hands of God.

To tell this story is in no way to minimize the terrible sorrow which that family experienced at the time of Ajit's death. Rather, the mother's words taught Dorothy and me to see our own lives in a much wider framework of meaning, hope and promise. What she said that night seemed to me to be a prophetic insight, yet for her they were quite natural words. In her spirituality there was no disconnection between this life and the new kind of life ahead. Although she had never heard of Jürgen Moltmann, she would have fully understood what his words meant. Certainly, if they had ever met up they could have had an amazingly joy-filled conversation!

Life itself, in all of its exuberance, contradiction, pain, searching and sheer goodness is also, as Moltmann reminds us, a 'fragment of death'. In my own journey, I have come to understand that Dorothy's authentic goodness which marked her days when she was in our midst, has now experienced enlargement in that dimension of God's purpose which Christians call the kingdom, even if I have difficulty with that particular word! It is this underlying fact of our 'continuity in God' which has brought my wounded spirit both comfort and challenge since that day when Dorothy's physical body was laid to rest among the Highland hills.

> O Christ, there is no plant in the ground
> But it is full of your virtue.
> There is no form in the strand
> But it is full of your blessing.
> There is no life in the sea,
> There is no creature in the ocean,
> There is nothing in the heavens
> But proclaims your goodness.

Finding Hope Again

There is no bird on the wing,
There is no star in the sky,
There is nothing beneath the sun,
But proclaims your goodness.

A Celtic prayer[26]

The smallest moment of hope

We believe in God
who takes our smallest moment of hope
and grows it forth like a tree
with spreading branches
for the sheltering of new life.

We believe in Jesus Christ
who walks tall among us,
seen in our faces, felt in our hearts,
bedded deep in the longing of our souls
for all that is true, just and full of hope.

We believe in the Holy Spirit
who waits on our moments of openness
and springs into the unknowns
with joy and delight,
that we might be called on
beyond where we thought we could go
where every step is walked on holy ground.

Dorothy McRae-McMahon[27]

The gift of tears

The Lord God drove out the man and sent him forth from the garden of Eden. And Eve was bitter and there was remorse in her soul. In her bitterness, as she followed in Adam's footsteps, legend tells us, she bit the top of the last leaf she passed on her way out through the gates, which is why the leaf of the tulip tree has a bite-shaped curve taken from it to this day.

There is another legend that the Lord God, seeing the remorse of Adam and his wife, was moved to pity. He repented of his hardness of heart and he spoke to them thus:

> My son, Adam, I can see thou and the woman that I gave thee have great sorrow. There is grief in your hearts for your transgression. In your life henceforth there will be enmity, adversity, and oppression, but I will give you solace. I have determined that you shall have a gift more precious than gold. It is this most costly pearl: a tear. When your souls are in pain and tribulation, when you are overcome by your grief, then shall this tear fall from your eyes and you shall be comforted and your burden shall be lightened.

When they heard the Lord God speak thus, Adam and his wife Eve were deeply grieved, and their eyes became fountains of tears which watered the earth. Since that day the seed of Adam and Eve have wept tears in their pain, and the pain has been eased.

A Jewish tale

Adam and Eve were given a precious gift – the ability to cry! I've had plenty of time to think about tears since Dorothy's death, and fortunately I don't find it difficult to shed them, although I know how hard it is for some of us to do that, even in the darkest nights.

Back in the days of the early church someone spoke of tears as being agents of resurrection and transformation. They had power within them. Another person called Isaac of Nineveh wrote: 'Whoever can weep over himself for one hour is greater than the one who is able to teach the whole world; whoever recognizes the depth of his own frailty is greater than the one who sees visions of angels!'

This idea that from our tears can burst forth new life is both a comfort and a challenge. Can we believe that tears are in fact a wonderful gift and their fruit can be joy? When Adam and Eve were able to cry, their pain was eased – their burdens were lifted. Is it the same for us who live at a time when oceans of tears are flowing through our world?

Sometimes we have to hit rock bottom to become fully alive. And in our lives there are various breakthroughs which take us to this place of helplessness. As we start to live out of our deepest longings and needs, we are, I am certain, brought home to God: the God who cries with us and who understands our suffering. Tears flow when the real source of life is uncovered, when our masks are off, when we have abandoned any strategies of self-deception. It's little wonder that they can be described as 'a gift'.

The sudden and totally unexpected death of someone

you love deeply propels you into this place of great power-lessness. You don't have a choice. You just are where you are – whatever that means! Without warning, you stand in a new place – in unfamiliar territory where tears ambush you from moment to moment. It's the rock-bottom place, and it's also the place where God is present.

I just hope that all my tears will lead me to a greater self-knowledge. I don't want them to be wasted! I would like to live gracefully with my wounds, with my power-lessness, with my inarticulate longings. Tears remind me that it is 'a waiting time' – and waiting times are often threaded through with fragility and uncertainty. Yet as I ponder on this old Jewish tale about Adam and Eve, I can begin to recognize that my tears are not only about help-lessness, for through them I may experience a restoration and renewal of my soul.

Mid-life blessing

May the blessing of the Maker be yours,
warmth and welcome and stars dancing in darkness,
circling you, cherishing you.

May the blessing of the Storyteller be yours,
justice and joy and bread for the journey,
challenging you, inspiring you.

May the blessing of the Holy Spirit be yours,
wind and fire and a bright shawl of wisdom,
disturbing you, comforting you.

May the blessing of friends and strangers be yours,
angels and saints and little ones playing,
encouraging you, befriending you.

Blessings be yours
in the midst of your journey;
may you be blessed with integrity and courage
in good times and bad times.

May you be strong and happy and creative.
May you be cradled and held in love.

Ruth Burgess[28]

Catching fire

I will not die an unlived life,
I will not go in fear
Of falling or catching fire.
I choose to inhabit my days,
To allow my living to open to me,
To make me less afraid,
More accessible,
To loosen my heart
Until it becomes a wing,
A torch, a promise.
I choose to risk my significance:
To live.
So that which comes to me as seed,
Goes to the next as blossom,
And that which came to me as blossom,
Goes on as fruit.

Davna Markova[29]

When Jesus met people they discovered liberation. They became less afraid, prepared to take risks. Open to life's extraordinary possibilities. More accessible to others. And their lives, as the gospel reminds us, 'bore fruit'.

In this powerful poem which was read at Dorothy's funeral service, Davna Markova takes us into this path where true liberation is discovered. It's about the invitation, announced in Scripture, to surrender our thoughts and actions into the hands of God – into that place from which true living flows. Essentially it's about 'letting go and letting God', which is a hard path for most of us in the modern world.

Many of the elements within modern culture militate against this idea of surrendering – of saying 'yes' to anything or anyone outside of our self-boundaried lives. We seek to guard our autonomy at all costs. We can live comfortably without 'giving over' our lives. In the film *About A Boy*, Hugh Grant plays Will, a rich, childless and irresponsible Londoner who, in the hunt for female conquests, invents an imaginary son and starts attending single-parents' meetings.

As a result of one of his liaisons, he meets Marcus, a bright, articulate, twelve-year-old misfit with problems at school and a suicidal mother. Gradually, Will and Marcus become friends, and as Will teaches Marcus how to be cool, Marcus helps Will to finally grow up. As Will begins to move out of his empty, affluent, self-enclosed existence in which shopping and no-strings sex were all that mattered, he starts to actually care about what is happening to Marcus. And as this caring develops, Will tells us that he has never felt happier and more at ease with himself.

It's easy to be cynical about a comedy-drama spun from the pages of Nick Hornby's best-selling novel. Yet *About A Boy* mirrors many dimensions in our society. Will was determined to live life to the sound of his own music, free of any relationships – to map out his days and nights with reference only to his own needs and desires. He divides his day into units with points attached to each – two for shopping, three for watching TV, two for being at the hair-dressers, three for sex, three for eating out, two for time at the gym and so on, until boredom overwhelms even the marking of the units!

And then Marcus explodes into this arid routine, and Will's life changes direction as he begins to reach out and to become involved with others. It's not an easy transition, accompanied as it is by endless domestic dramas. But in the end Will goes in for risk-taking, for catching fire.

The film made me think about any situation where I would be willing, as Davna Markova put it, 'to risk my significance in order to live'. Yet is that not exactly what the gospel calls forth from us? Christ did not invite the people he encountered into some comfortable club. He called them into a place of transformation, of new beginnings, of surprise. A place where the boundaries would not be known, and in which there might not be any security. A place where you might actually catch fire or fall into the unknown.

And that comes back to this belief in inner liberation, which runs through not only Christianity but all the great religions of the world. The surrendering of self in order to love. To me that seems like an incredibly vast vision for a fragile person, and perhaps I should heed Desmond Tutu's wisdom when he says that an elephant can only be eaten in small pieces. These amazing characters who met Jesus in the flesh only got a glimmer of what it was all about – of that I'm certain. But it was enough. Because of meeting him, their hearts were loosened, and they sensed what they were truly to be on this earth – liberated and healed companions of God.

A season of feasting

On the Sunday before her death, Dorothy was leading worship in our village church. It was the start of Lent, and she invited the congregation to meditate on these words which she had found on a Benedictine website. The following day, she e-mailed this meditation to friends in various parts of the world. She found the words affirming because they celebrated the glorious gift of renewed life in Christ, while at the same time making practical suggestions about daily living!

In her introduction to the meditation Dorothy said: 'Lent can be more than a time of fasting: it can be a season of feasting. We can use Lent to fast from certain things and to feast on others. It is a season in which we can . . .'

Fast from judging others: feast on the Christ dwelling
  in them
Fast from emphasis on differences: feast on the unity
  of life
Fast from apparent darkness: feast on the reality of light
Fast from thoughts of illness: feast on the healing power
  of God
Fast from words that pollute: feast on phrases that purify
Fast from discontent: feast on gratitude
Fast from anger: feast on patience
Fast from pessimism: feast on optimism

Fast from worry: feast on divine order
Fast from complaining: feast on appreciation
Fast from negatives: feast on affirmatives
Fast from unrelenting pressures: feast on unceasing prayer
Fast from hostility: feast on non-resistance
Fast from bitterness: feast on forgiveness
Fast from self-concern: feast on compassion for others
Fast from personal anxiety: feast on eternal truth
Fast from discouragements: feast on hope
Fast from facts that depress: feast on verities that uplift
Fast from lethargy: feast on enthusiasm
Fast from thoughts that weaken: feast on promises that
    inspire
Fast from shadows of sorrow: feast on the sunlight of
    serenity
Fast from idle gossip: feast on purposeful silence.[30]

Oran's Chapel

Oran's Chapel on the Hebridean island of Iona has a special place in my heart. It was built in the twelfth century and restored in the twentieth. The chapel itself stands within the Reilig Odhrain (Oran's graveyard). Oran was a cousin of Columba, and was reputedly the first of his monks to die and be buried on the island. From the ninth century to the eleventh, the Reilig Odhrain was a royal burial ground for Scottish and Norse kings, and also for local chieftains.

Each week the Iona Community organizes a pilgrimage around Iona, visiting its many sacred and historic sites. This walking pilgrimage ends with prayers and singing in Oran's Chapel. Some people may think it strange that the pilgrimage should end in a graveyard, but throughout Christian history burial grounds have been seen as places of resurrection – of new hope. It was in a burial place that, twenty centuries ago, the resurrection faith began.

I have had the privilege of leading the Iona pilgrimage many times. When the group of pilgrims arrived at Oran's Chapel they were often tired – as the walk takes several hours, often over rough ground. Usually we were a large number, particularly in the warmer months and, on most weeks, from several different countries. Some of the group would have described themselves as committed Christians, others as seekers on the edge of institutional religion, while others would not regard themselves as in either of these categories. It is this vibrant mixture of human beings, young and old, rich and poor who, week by week, make the Iona pilgrimage a very special event for literally thousands of people every year.

At the end of our walk, once we were gathered within the stout walls of this ancient chapel, no matter how weary we might be, we seemed to forget our physical needs as we shared together in silence, spoken prayer and sometimes singing. It was always an expectant atmosphere, even on those days of torrential rain and mist-shrouded hills! People knew that the pilgrimage was ending, but they also felt that the kaleidoscope of experiences which the day had brought would remain with them for a long time.

Over the years, the Iona Community, in its understanding of this island pilgrimage, has rightly seen that although the arrival at Oran's Chapel marks the end of the day's walking, it is also symbolizes what lies ahead for the pilgrims. It is therefore viewed not just as a historic building but also as a powerful 'place of sending' from which we go out to continue the ongoing mission and ministry of Christ throughout the world. The chapel, in these final moments of the Iona pilgrimage, becomes a space in which we can recommit ourselves both to God and to the world. And after our prayers, as we step out through its ancient carved doorway, to go our separate ways, God's blessing, which enfolded Columba and his monks 1,500 years ago, propels us to invite fresh vision for ourselves.

It's this ever-present challenge which has made Oran's Chapel a significant marker in my own faith journey. As one prayer from Uganda puts it: 'Holy Spirit, give us faith, give us hope, give us love and revive your work in this land, beginning with me.' It's about this truth at the heart of Christ's message which tells us that we will always be pilgrims, walking in a provisional way on the earth. Lightly, with no continuing city. Yet even as pilgrims always on the move, we walk by faith, and, as the letter to the Hebrews says, to have faith 'is to be sure of the things we hope for, to be certain of the things we cannot see' (Hebrews 11:1).

Even when I am far away from the west coast of Scotland, I visualize Oran's Chapel on the rocky island of Iona as a 'place of sending' from which we can move on in hope. But I also realize that these places which give us fresh courage and vision for the journey are not just to be found in famous places of pilgrimage. They are everywhere around, and speak to us at many levels of our being. And they can be trees or hillsides or rivers as much as buildings.

Several years ago, a group of us opened a Citizens' Advice Bureau in my parish in the East End of Glasgow. The Bureau was not situated in some modern, well-designed building, but occupied a first-floor flat in a tenement block that was in its final days. Everything about the building was run-down, and the desks and files were crammed into the smallest of spaces. Yet within weeks of the Bureau's opening, I knew we were in a sacred space – a place both of sending and of healing. The walls of that shabby office reverberated day after day with stories of courage, love, pain and violence, but through them all glimmered life-giving signs of the gospel.

There were no formal prayers of the kind shared week by week in Oran's Chapel, but the CAB was a place of prayer just the same. Every time I went there, I came away restored in spirit and more determined than ever to be aware of the human pain and joy which marked daily life in Glasgow's impoverished East End. I came away a humbler and more centred person. The many families and individuals who came to the Bureau were always teaching me new things about God and life. Despite the poverty of its setting, or maybe because of it, that place was a centre of hope, a place of sending.

When we left Glasgow, we went to live and work in India, and there many village homes – simple thatched huts – became for me important 'sending places'. I loved being in them, and sharing rice with the families whose forebears had been in the same place for hundreds of years. Every day brought new hardships for these folk who were on the margins of society. They were the victims of centuries of horrific injustice, yet their trust in God's goodness never seemed to leave them. When we visited them, they would offer us what was literally their last bite, without any thought that they would go hungry if we took the food.

Even when up against constant financial struggle and illness, the villagers of South India were people of the heart who understood life's sacred mystery. Their close connection to the soil enlarged their practical spirituality, and with centuries of tradition behind them they recognized in the face of the stranger, the face of God. To be a guest in a village home was an honour, and I know that through this hospitality, I began to understand more about the sacred in myself. When I came away from their homes, I knew I was leaving with a greater awareness of God. I had been in another kind of 'sending place' – a place in which I had found new direction for my life, and renewed hope for what lay ahead.

Which brings me back to Oran's Chapel. When I was living in Iona Abbey I would often walk the short distance over to the chapel, late at night. In it a single candle would be burning, and I would just sit there in the silence, on a mat on the stone floor. Sometimes I thought about very little, allowing the silence to carry its multiple messages. At other times I thought about all the people who had been inside the chapel during the day. All of them had made the long journey to Iona, and some had travelled thousands of miles. And with them they brought the rich and incredible stories of their lives.

Some may have been in the chapel only for a few moments, others for hours. Some may have come with a deep faith in God, others with little or none. Yet I knew that their lives would have been touched in some way by coming to this tiny house of prayer. I also hoped that they would discover many other 'sending places' as they travelled on. Places where they could pause and discover that God was a much larger reality than they had ever imagined, and that he was continually offering the gift of hope in remarkable ways. Just as I discovered when I went into that Citizens' Advice Bureau in Glasgow, or visited those welcoming homes beneath the palms and close to the paddy fields in the villages of South India.

And all of this is beautifully expressed in words which come from South Africa. There they are used as a blessing on the people as they go from church, facing again the myriad journeys in their lives. Yet they reach much further than a local congregation in South Africa, for they carry hope, illumination and grace for us all:

We must move on,
my people!

This is merely a resting place,
a place of transit,
where humanity and God pause
before taking the road again.

Go, my people,
you are ready to set sail,
your country is not here.

You are a wayfaring people,
strangers, never rooted in one place,
pilgrims moving towards an abiding city further on.

Go forth, my people,
go and pray further off,
love will be your song,
and life your celebration.
Go, you are the house of God,
stones cut according to the measure of God's love.

You are awaited, my people,
and I declare to you, people of God,
I am going with you.[31]

God's blessing

I bless the poverty in your heart, that knows
its own emptiness, because that gives me
space to grow my Kingdom there.

I bless that in you that touches others gently,
because everyone responds to gentleness,
and gentleness can capture even hardened hearts.

I bless that in you which grieves and aches for
all that is lost or can never be, because that
is my opportunity to comfort you with my,
much greater, love.

I bless that in you which longs and strives
after your own deepest truth and after
truth for the world, because even as you
pray I am constantly satisfying these deep
unspoken longings.

I bless you every time you show mercy
and forgiveness, because that is like a little
window in your heart, setting you free from
resentment and opening up a space for me
to enter and to heal.

I bless the purity of your heart, because that
is the elusive centre where your deepest

desire meets mine. That is where we meet
face to face.

I bless the peacemaker in you – that in your soul
which seeks the peace that passeth understanding,
even at a great cost.

I bless even those things in your experience
of journeying with me that feel like
persecution and misunderstanding because they are
   the proof
that your faith is no illusion.

Margaret Silf[32]

Recovering our secret name

As I think back on my life, hidden in the secret recesses of my heart-memory, I discover or, perhaps, feel those who accepted and loved me just as I was. They did not judge me: there was unconditional love. One of those people who freed me to be more fully who I was and am was Father Thomas Philippe. It was he who introduced me to people with intellectual disabilities and who helped me to see their value and importance in the world, for they are people of the heart. As I experience him today in my heart-memory I feel waters of forgiveness and goodness flowing from him, waters that refresh and help me regain trust in myself and in my secret name, that is to say, my mission in life, the reason I was born. Father Thomas was truly free and he in turn, freed others. Maybe once in our life we will be fortunate enough to meet such a person.

Jean Vanier[33]

On the uphill road to discover hope again, each of us needs someone like Jean Vanier's friend, Father Thomas. And somewhere deep inside me I believe that God gives us such a person – often in surprising ways. Not just to comfort and hold us, but to bring the gift of fresh vision to our lives: to remind us that one day the clouds will lift.

And these people who accept us as we are and help us to be more fully alive, don't usually step onto our path in any planned way. They arrive unannounced, and they intuitively know where we are at that moment.

And as they walk with us, slowly but surely, they reveal to us our 'secret name'. Through their insight and open compassion they are able to take us into the depths of our being, allowing us to gently confront the hurt and anguish which may be governing our thoughts and actions. It's a mystery how this happens and analysing it does not help! Tenderly, they announce a great truth about our existence on this earth – that we have been loved by God from before the beginning of time. They remind us that we have a special story going on inside. A story to celebrate.

The philosopher Martin Buber, in his book *The Road of Mankind* wrote: 'with each person who comes into the world, there is something new that has never existed before, something totally new and unique. It is this unique and exceptional quality that each person is called to develop.' When we lose hope in ourselves, we forget this and are unable to celebrate our rich humanness. I know this is true for me. Yet when I am with a person or people who accept me as I am and love me warts and all, I can begin to return to that space within me where new hope is born.

Time and again in the Gospels, Jesus did this very thing – freeing women and men to discover their true selves: to discover their heart. Folk who carried very little sense of worth in themselves were suddenly brought into their full humanity because they had met Jesus on the road. They never expected this kind of transformation – it came as a gift, a surprise. And sometimes they only recognized it as time went on. There was a gradual evolution into a different person.

As I look back on my own journey, I recognize that I have always been attracted by these stories in the Bible in which ordinary women and men begin to see who they really are, because God has touched their lives. This encounter with God propels them into a new place from which their understanding of reality is transformed. We sometimes use the word 'conversion' to describe this change. Whatever word is used, it is this discovery of our 'secret name' in God – our purpose in living – which allows us to experience that kind of hope about which Paul wrote in his letter to the small church in Corinth (1 Corinthians 13).

And as we move closer to who we actually are, devoid of our masks, Christ's hope can take root in our souls even when outward circumstances are bleak. When people begin to discover their 'secret name' because of their encounter with Jesus, they are, literally, restored; they have 'come home' to that place in which God's Spirit can permeate their living. At the weekly healing service in Iona Abbey we often use a powerful prayer which, for me, captures a central truth within this recovery of our true self in God:

> Spirit of the living God,
> present with us now,
> enter you, body, mind and spirit,
> and heal you of all that harms you,
> in Jesus' name.

The entering of God's Spirit into our whole being – not just into parts of us. These words are strong – 'body', 'mind', 'spirit' – but it is so affirming that they carry this strength, for it means we are encountering the mystery of God's presence, and not just some small god of our own devising. This is the living Christ whose light pierces even our darkest nights and who offers wholeness with such amazing tenderness.

In my own fragility, I believe that recovering my 'secret name' – my true purpose in life, the reason why I am on earth – is an absolutely fundamental step in my rediscovering not only hope, but also faith and love. For as the Bible tells us, these three are interconnected in the heart of God. As I respond to the promptings of my hidden, inner life, I can move in one of two directions. On the one hand, I can move further and further into a self-enclosed existence, forgetting that I'm stamped with God's image, or, on the other, I can say 'yes' to the One whose Spirit enfolds me.

Brother Roger, founder of the Taizé Community in France, who has seen into many hearts, and perhaps especially the hearts of young people who are searching for meaning in their lives, once wrote about the imperceptible changes that take place in us as we discover who we truly are in God: 'It is the fact of looking towards the invisible Christ that determines the transformation of our whole being. These changes may be imperceptible, and they are better so; it is enough to know that by night and by day the seed takes root and grows without our knowing how.'[34]

> Lord,
> you know what burdens us,
> and
> when our fears rule us,
> when our self-worth disappears,

Christ's Hope

when failures overwhelm,
when relationships collapse,
when our bodies cry out in pain,
when our minds are tormented,
when our tears can flow no more,
you speak our secret name,
and welcome us home.

A moment of revealing

Some words sent by a friend:

> I believe I am created in the image of God.
> I believe God delights in me.
>
> I believe God invites me to move
> From compulsion to choice;
> To listen to my inner voice
> And seek wisdom;
> To speak my truth.
>
> I believe God
> Empowers me to
> Share with others
> The journey to wholeness.
>
> I believe the gifts I have are God-given –
> To be used fully and generously.
> As I do this, I will become
> All I am intended to be.
>
> I believe God calls me
> Into creative relationships –
> With others as with myself;
> To love and be loved;
> To hold pain and potential –
> Mine and others.

Christ's Hope

I believe I am called
To a mature independence
Which enables authentic community.

I believe in a creating God
Who at this very moment
Is revealing
A new thing.

I believe God
Stands with me now.

I believe God
Has brought me
To this place.

Foundations of hope

I ask God from the wealth of his glory to give you power through his Spirit to be strong in your inner selves, and I pray that Christ will make his home in your hearts through faith. I pray that you may have your roots and foundation in love, so that you, together with all God's people, may have the power to understand how broad and long, how high and deep is Christ's love. Yes, may you come to know his love – although it can never be fully known – and so be completely filled with the very nature of God.

To him who by means of his power working in us is able to do much more than we can ever ask for, or even think of: to God be glory in the church and in Christ Jesus for all time, for ever and ever!

Ephesians 3 : 14–21

Perhaps more than any other passage in the Bible, these words of Paul to the Christians in Ephesus have given me renewed hope. That does not mean I understand them! Far from it. It will take a few more thousand years before human beings, however diligent in their theology, will be able to unpack the mystery, healing, wisdom and transformative power held within them. Yet they speak to me with clarity, and tell of a God who, I believe, companions my existence on earth. I have read them in my darkest moments, and been brought back to light, but what exactly that means I will never know, for the movements of our heart are in themselves a mystery.

There are several reasons why I find these words so hope-filled. Even glancing at them, they immediately lift me away from any idea of 'a small god'. I read here about the Creator and Sustainer of the universe – and that's a long, long way from a domesticated god who, as some imagine, spends all his time keeping them blessed and free from hassle! Rather, this is a God of limitless mystery who has also, in tenderness, given a sign of him or herself within our fragile human condition.

As I try to find hope again, Paul confronts me with a Christ who invites me to experience something beyond my imagining. It's almost impossible to grasp the many dimensions opened up by this invitation. I am being asked in my vulnerability and unsteady faith, to touch into the Creator's energy: to journey into my depths and to discover that at the core of my being Christ's Spirit resides. To awaken to a truth which is, that through faith, however wobbly it may be, Christ has made his home – yes, his home! – in my heart, through love. It's mind-blowing stuff, but when the chips are down, I believe in its truth, even if its implications are well beyond my grasp!

As I open my life out to the truth that a God-given energy is at work within me, then it follows that I can access greater inner strength. Strength to love, to hope, to be the person God wants me to be. And what is so compelling about this God is that in Christ he refused to short-circuit his own humanity. He became 'flesh of our flesh'. The One who makes 'his home in our hearts' – has also experienced these dark tunnels that engulf us. He is no stranger to the agonies of rejection, fear and loneliness. Tessa Sheaf, in her book. *How I Pray*, expresses this in words which I find immensely helpful:

It is when I look at the lives of the people around me – often fellow divorcees – who have also wept, sweated blood and somehow crawled out of their prisons that I realize the life of each one of us is 'holy ground' where God is mysteriously wiping our tears, mending the rubble of our broken lives and leading us from darkness to light. It is then that I want to sing like Mary, 'My soul magnifies the Lord, my spirit rejoices in God my Saviour', for then I know he does not abandon us.[35]

And that small group of believers in Ephesus all those centuries ago were also reminded that we would never begin to fathom the greatness of this enfolding Love. All we could do was walk within it, or run towards it, or swim in it, or turn our wheelchairs in its direction! For, believe it or not, it was a free gift. And if it were ever given a price-tag it would be lost – which is a real problem for those who are convinced you don't get anything for nothing! The old hymn was right when it said: 'amazing Love so full and free', for it is amazing and is so freely offered. And in its embrace we learn of our own sacredness.

Yet it has always been impossible for me to believe that this incredible free-flowing Love is to be discovered only among Christians. God is much bigger than the churches, for which we must be thankful as we reflect on the rather scarred history of institutional religion! In my own life I am committed to the Church, for I know that along with its flaws are great treasures, especially the people.

But in recent years I have become disappointed that

many Christians refuse to believe that there is anything of God's love and purpose in the other great world religions. They only see them as 'areas of darkness' from which people must be 'rescued'.

The Ephesians passage, however, raises this central question – Where do we see God's Spirit at work in the modern world? Or, in what ways is Christ's Spirit present in our midst today? Mother Teresa kept telling us that in the faces of the poorest people on earth, whatever their religion, we see the face of Jesus Christ. She herself was committed to Christianity but through years of disciplined prayer she came to recognize that the Spirit of Jesus was in the lives of people who did not even know his name. She knew that there was a Love at work in this world – higher, broader and deeper than our limited human imagining.

As I read Paul's words, it becomes clear to me that Christians have to be humble about the working of God's Spirit. The Gospel of John reminds us that we don't know where 'the wind of the Spirit blows'. Sometimes in India, visiting Christian evangelists would tell us that they were there to 'bring the gospel'. They were free to do that. But while preaching about Christ's love, could they not also have taken time to learn a little about Hinduism – a faith which has sustained literally hundreds of millions of people for thousands of years? But for them Hinduism had nothing to do with God, and they had nothing to learn from it.

There is the story of the Hindu who said to the Christian: 'For you God is up there, but for me God is in here', as he pointed to his heart. Of course both understandings are true, and both are limited. And as I try to rediscover the foundations of ultimate hope, both for myself and for our world, I feel comfortable with the truth that God will never be contained in our definitions, and my journey into God will go on long after my breathing has stopped.

When we lived in India, the Benedictine monk Bede Griffiths, who died some years ago, was not only a friend but a spiritual guide, as he was to thousands of others. He loved this section of Ephesians, because he knew that the tremendous power of the Spirit is abroad in the world today in many new and exciting ways. He wrote:

> The whole Bible grew over nearly two thousand years, as the whole church has grown over these two thousand years. This growing process involves allowing the Holy Spirit to open the mind to the deeper dimensions of reality, of Truth, and of the deep meaning of the Bible. We can pray that the Holy Spirit enlightens us all to receive that deeper understanding to see what God is doing to us in the world today.[36]

I find immense reservoirs of hope in this conviction that the Spirit is constantly leading us into deeper dimensions of reality, of Truth. Surely this belief must have been in the mind of Paul when he wrote: 'his power working in you is able to do so much more than we can ever ask for, or even think of'. And is one of these greater things, which God is doing in our time, about inviting us into a more profound sense of hope?

As we live through this time of conflict, disintegration and disillusionment, can our minds be opened to understand our global situation with a more truly engaged compassion? To believe as one writer put it, 'that in a dark time, the eye begins to see'. That may seem a hard vision at a time when there are not only rumours of war, but many actual wars. It may seem difficult to believe as we destroy more and more of the natural world. It may seem like a crazy vision in a period when millions get richer and richer, and millions more become poorer and poorer.

Yet rebirth is present, and in the midst of our present global chaos, there is a reawakening of hearts. It is not something I only read about. It is something which I see around me, and around the world. God's Spirit is moving in our midst in strange, exciting and uncomfortable ways. God is 'at home' in many hearts, as Paul said all those years ago. And that knowledge is one of the foundations for my own recovery of hope.

> At Christ's table we offer the Bread,
> that Bread which carries all
> the bewilderment,
> the anguish,
> the blood,
> the pain,
> the injustice,
> the poverty,
> the hate,
> the anger,
> the fear,
> the death,
> the bombs,
> and we offer it
> for peace, for transfiguration, for compassion,
> for Shalom
> at the heart of the world.
>
> *Desmond Tutu*

The Spirit's surprises

May the Spirit
bless you with discomfort
at easy answers, half-truths and
superficial relationships so that
you will live deep in your heart.

May the Spirit
bless you with anger
at injustice and oppression,
and exploitation of people and the earth
so that you will work for
justice, equity and peace.

May the Spirit
bless you with tears to shed
for those who suffer
so that you will
reach out your hand
to comfort them.

And may the Spirit
bless you with the foolishness
to think you can make a difference
in the world,
so you will do the things
which others say cannot be done.

Interfaith Council for Peace and Justice[37]

192

Notes

1. From Michael Leunig, *A Common Prayer* (Collins Dove, 1990).
2. A prayer used during Christian Aid Week.
3. Jean Vanier, *Becoming Human* (Darton, Longman and Todd, 2001), pp. 85–6.
4. Archbishop Rowan Williams in a pamphlet published in 2001 by the Christian Socialist Movement (1st Floor, Bradley Close, White Lion Street, London N1 9PF).
5. Henry Longfellow, from his poem 'Hyperion' (1839).
6. Vaclav Havel, *Living in Truth* (Faber and Faber, London, 1987).
7. Basil Hume, *The Mystery of the Incarnation* (Darton, Longman and Todd, 1999).
8. Quoted in Dorothy Millar, *Seeds for the Morrow* (published privately, 2001).
9. Obituary in *The Independent*, 21 February 2001.
10. Dr Sandy Locke, article in 'Personal View' column, *British Medical Journal*, Vol. 322, 6 January 2000.
11. Rabindranath Tagore, *Gitanjali*, Part XXIX (Macmillan, India, 1985).
12. From the magazine of Manvers Baptist Church, Bath.
13. Neil Paynter (ed.), *Lent and Easter Readings from Iona* (Wild Goose Publications, 2001), pp. 110–12.
14. Kahlil Gibran, *The Prophet* (Heinemann, 1964).
15. Archbishop Desmond Tutu, Preface to Nelson Mandela's *Long Walk to Freedom* (Abacus, 1996).
16. Nelson Mandela, *Long Walk to Freedom*.
17. Alex Logan, article in *Coracle*, the magazine of the Iona Community, Spring 2001.

18. Quoted in Millar, *Seeds for the Morrow*.
19. James Mawdsley, article in *The Methodist Recorder*, April 2002.
20. Published in *Letter from Taizé*, February/March 1999.
21. From Janet Morley (ed.), *Bread for the Morrow* (SPCK/Christian Aid, 1992).
22. From Alexander Carmichael (ed.), *Carmina Gadelica* (Floris Books, 1994).
23. From *The Taizé Letter*, February/March 1999.
24. From Jürgen Moltmann, *The Open Church* (SCM Press, 1978).
25. From Carmichael, *Carmina Gadelica*.
26. From *The Iona Community Worship Book* (Wild Goose Publications, 1994).
27. From *Liturgies for the Journey of Life* (SPCK, 2000).
28. From Ruth Burgess, *A Book of Blessings* (Wild Goose Publications, 2001), p. 56.
29. From *Coracle*, the magazine of the Iona Community.
30. From the website of the Benedictine Community, Lent 2001.
31. Quoted in Morley, *Bread for the Morrow*.
32. From Margaret Silf, *Landmarks: An Ignatian Journey* (Darton, Longman and Todd, 1998).
33. Vanier, *Becoming Human*, p. 101.
34. From *A Letter to Taizé*, Spring 2000.
35. Tessa Sheaf, *How I Pray*, ed. John Wilkins (Darton, Longman and Todd, 1993).
36. Bede Griffiths, *The New Creation in Christ* (Darton, Longman and Todd, 1992).
37. Interfaith Council for Peace and Justice, Ann Arbor, Michigan.